Planning the quality of education

Planning the quality of education

The collection and use of data for informed decision-making

Edited by
Kenneth N. Ross
and
Lars Mählck

Unesco: International Institute for Educational Planning
Pergamon Press

English language edition first co-published in 1990 by the
United Nations Educational, Scientific and Cultural Organization,
7 place de Fontenoy, 75700 Paris, France and
Pergamon Press plc, Headington Hill Hall, Oxford, England.
Printed in France by Imprimerie Gauthier-Villars, 75018 Paris

Unesco ISBN 92-803-1139-5 (Limp-bound edition)
Pergamon ISBN 0-08-041026X (Hard-back edition)
© Unesco 1990

This volume includes contributions by:

Abdel Ghani Al-nouri
Arfah A. Aziz
Zolthan Bathory
Boediono
Jean-Pierre Boisivon
Etienne Brunswic
Gabriel Carceles Breis
Kiran Dhingra
Mats Ekholm
Viola Esponola
Bruce Fuller
Dorothy M. Gilford
Aletta Grisay
Jacques Hallak
Stephen P. Heyneman
Archie Lapointe
Henry M. Levin
Marlaine E. Lockheed
Lars Mählck
Kilemi Mwiria
T. Neville Postlethwaite
Colin N. Power
Kenneth N. Ross
Anthony Somerset
Douglas M. Windham

Preface

This book was prepared from the papers and discussions associated with an international workshop on *Issues and Practices in Planning the Quality of Education* that was organised by the International Institute for Educational Planning in November 1989. The workshop represented the third in a series covering two decades that have aimed to re-shape the directions of educational planning in accordance with the prevailing social and economic challenges faced by educational systems.

The first workshop (Beeby, 1969) was centred around a philosophical debate that sought to clarify the concept of "the quality of education" and then to explore its relationships with the field of educational planning. The second workshop (Adams, 1978) was more pragmatic and judgemental in nature as it scrutinised the uneven patterns of success that educational planners had experienced in seeking to improve the quality of education.

This third workshop, while building upon the earlier contributions, has examined the major issues surrounding the collection and use of information by educational planners for the purpose of improving the quality of education through informed decision-making.

A major achievement of this workshop has been to develop an agenda for international action that was designed to foster improvements in the collection and use of educational information. The agenda, which included a list of fundamental research, training, and co-operation needs in the field of educational planning, can be addressed successfully provided that concerted and co-ordinated efforts are made at both national and international levels.

The International Institute for Educational Planning would like to express its thanks to the workshop participants for their contributions to the book. In particular, thanks are due to Professor T.N. Postlethwaite for his Chairmanship of the workshop proceedings, and also his many contributions to the design and preparation of the book.

June 1990

Jacques Hallak
Director, IIEP

Contents

Introduction

Chapter 1

A new mission for educational planning[1]

Overview of the book

In November 1989, the International Institute for Educational Planning organized an invitational workshop focussed on *Issues and Practices in Planning the Quality of Education.* The workshop was attended by an international panel of educational administrators, planners, and researchers. The workshop participants were asked to address the theme that *"Planning the quality of education through informed decision-making requires the availability of accurate and timely information that links together resource inputs to education, teaching-learning conditions and processes, and appropriate indicators of the knowledge, skills, and values acquired by students."*

The workshop activities were mainly centred around the preparation of a series of papers on key sub-areas of the overall workshop theme. The papers were designed to present international viewpoints of educational planning with reference to primary and secondary education. This book was based primarily on these papers, however, it also includes a considerable amount of material arising from the many lively discussions that occurred among the workshop participants as their papers were being prepared and then reported in plenary sessions.

---

1. This chapter was prepared by Kenneth Ross and Lars Mählck.

The book consists of three main parts. The first part considers the different information requirements for different levels of decision making in education, and then moves to a review of established educational information collection practices. The second part explores the linkages betwen information and the quality of education -- providing arguments that illustrate how the design of educational information systems must start with a clear analysis of the "interests" of decision-makers. The third part illustrates two areas where many countries have experienced difficulties in the collection and use of educational information: the dialogue between the producers and consumers of information, and the technical issues associated with the collection, preparation, and analysis of information.

The conclusion to the book summarizes the fundamental needs for training and research that emerged from the preceding chapters. The needs were grouped under six headings and some proposals for responding to them were presented. These proposals, taken together, constitute a large-scale attack on many important issues in educational planning and will therefore require a co-ordinated international effort in order to ensure their successful implementation.

"Planning the quality of education": the interpretation accepted for this book

In situations where the word "quality" is used in a descriptive sense it simply refers to the possession, or not, of an attribute. Therefore, in this sense, the use of the word to describe an object is relatively uncontroversial. That is, a person can be described as "having certain qualities" without implying anything about comparisons or value judgements. However, difficulties often arise when the word is used to describe an object in an evaluative sense that implies some underlying scale of "goodness". That is, a person may be described as a "a high quality person", and accordingly it might be said that the person is "better" in comparison with other people. The difficulty in this context is that, in order to understand the meaning of the word, a clear specification of the nature of the underlying scale is required.

To add to these difficulties, when the word "quantity" also enters the discussion, the supplementary task usually arises of disentangling and then explaining a commonly perceived dichotomy between "quantity" and "quality". This perceived dichotomy arises because, in everyday language, the two words are often used with the word "or" placed, or implied, between them. A common example of this type of usage occurs when people discuss a "qualitative assessment" of an object in order to signify that the assessment was "not quantitative" in the sense that it was subjective, judgmental, holistic, and not based on the measurement of identifiable parts.

The International Institute for Educational Planning has held two previous conferences (Beeby, 1969, Adams, 1978) that were concerned with the concept of "quality" when it is applied to the field of education. It makes absorbing reading to place the first conference report, dominated by philosophers and social scientists who wanted to "straighten out" the definitions of "quality" versus "quantity", beside the second conference report that was dominated by pragmatists who saw it to be more pertinent to ask why there was a need for this kind of dichotomy -- either at the definitional level or especially at the workface where most Ministries of Education had separated, intellectually and physically, the activities that generally fell under the heading of "provision" (quantity) from those that generally fell under the heading "outcomes" (quality). A major highlight of the first conference was the address given by the "Minister of Education of Ruatoria" who indicated that he had a number of questions that required satisfactory answers before he would commit his developing country to the pursuit of an improvement in the quality of education. In the following extract it is possible to recognize that at the heart of his uncertainty was the requirement that a range of value judgements needed to be made in order to come to terms with the notion of quality.

"Underlying all the discussions in this symposium was the assumption that the concept of quality in education is relative, that, standing by itself, the term is devoid of meaning. In his paper Peters (1969) insists that there are 'multiple criteria of quality', and that one must always ask the question 'Good for what?'. Philp (1969) goes further when he says that it is impossible to discuss the quality of a school system without first knowing its goals, which must be based, in turn, on the goals society has set for itself. No one can quarrel with this theory of Philp, but where does it leave

5

me as an administrator? I would gladly base the aims of a system on the goals of society, but who is to tell me what they are? Society, as I know it as a politician in a democratic country, is a hydra-headed monster that speaks with many tongues. (Beeby, 1969, p. 47).

In a later incarnation, as Professor C. E. Beeby, the Minister came to a similar conclusion concerning the impossibility of preparing an absolute definition of quality. He therefore decided to adopt a less controversial position by putting forward the term "qualitative change" by initially distinguishing it from "quantitative change". The latter term was defined as "a simple linear expansion, or diminution, of current practice, more -- or less -- of what already exists: more buildings, more students and teachers, fewer examinations of the present type and standards" (Beeby, 1979, p. 17). Beeby defined "qualitative change" along two dimensions: "qualitative change in the classroom" -- *what* is taught and *how* it is taught, and "qualitative change in the flow of students" -- *who* is taught and *where* he/she is taught (Beeby, 1979, p 17).

During the latter part of the 1980s, there has been considerable semantic and philosophical debate about the meaning of the term "quality of education" (see, for example, the extensive review of terminology prepared by OECD (1989)). However, it would appear that few analyses have pushed the definition beyond Beeby's elegant and, importantly, usable operationalization. Therefore, following due consideration of the above discussion, and in full understanding of the impossible task of reaching complete agreement concerning an absolute definition, it was decided to reserve the notion of "quality" during the workshop meetings in which this book was written to describe the matters that came within the realm of what Beeby defined as "qualitative change in the classroom". That is, the phrase *"planning the quality of education"* was interpreted as being concerned with educational planning that was likely to result in an improvement in the environment in which the student worked with the aids to learning provided for that purpose by the school system, and that this improved environment could reasonably be expected to express itself as detectable gains in the knowledge, skills, and values acquired by students.

Educational planning: past present and future

The planning of education on a major scale has taken place in various countries since early this century when some exposure to formal primary schooling came to be seen as being appropriate for the majority of children. It was in the 1960s, however, that an international emphasis was given to the field of educational planning as most countries -- both developed and developing -- commenced to pursue the goal of ever-increasing participation rates in primary and secondary education. The pursuit of continuous growth in enrolments resulted in planners being concerned primarily with the expansion of educational provision in terms of buildings, equipment, and manpower. This early mission was re-focussed on several occasions throughout the 1970s and 1980s, and the 1990s has commenced with educational planners needing to provide evidence to decision-makers to show that increasingly scarce resources will be deployed in cost-effective ways that are likely to improve the quality of education for *all* students.

In broad terms there have been three major eras in educational planning since the 1960s. The following discussion describes these eras and then suggests a "new mission" for educational planners in the 1990s.

A comfortable era: planning for expansion

In the early 1960s, many developing countries were beginning to look optimistically towards the prospect of achieving universal primary schooling. Accordingly, they sought information to design strategies in which the resources required to achieve that goal could be acquired and then put into action. At the same time, the industrialized countries were afforded the luxury of contemplating how to expand enrolments in post-compulsory schooling, and how to ensure that the number of new graduates from this sector was sufficient to meet the requirements of continued economic growth. These wealthier countries had also become engaged by the emerging belief that participation in education was an intrinsically worthwhile activity and that access to it should be distributed equitably across all socially-defined groups.

In this setting, educational planners around the world became preoccupied with strategies that would facilitate the delivery of "educational inputs" in terms of personnel, accommodation, and equipment. The emphasis in their work was on the speed and coverage of delivery, with little concern being expressed about whether this large-scale mobilization of resources would establish the kinds of conditions that would lead to an improvement in "educational outputs" -- especially those associated with student learning.

This was an extremely comfortable era for educational planners. Their mission, "the expansion of schooling", was unequivocal, and their working methodologies, collectively described by Coombs (1975: p. 17) as the "numbers game", were established and unchallenged. In addition, new plans for growth in education systems were usually received by governments without question, except perhaps on the grounds of finance. These plans were generally straightforward in intention, unobtrusive in implementation, and the means for evaluating them were self-evident and ready at hand.

A *loss of innocence: research-based challenges for educational planning*

Just when things were moving along nicely, the research findings of the legendary "Equality of Educational Opportunity" study (Coleman et al. (1966)) started to spoil the fun. The study, inspired partly by a concern for the disparity in educational provision in the United States between the wealthy northern states and the poorer southern states, set out to measure educational inputs to schools and then to consider, after controlling statistically for the home environments of students, which of these inputs could best explain variation between schools with respect to student achievement. In the mid 1960s, from an educational planner's perspective, this seemed a very sensible and thrifty way of deriving a short list of "effective" educational inputs. In fact, the study appeared to be the answer to a planner's dreams because it seemed to have the potential to answer all those nagging questions about which items needed to be provided for schools in order for all students to obtain a good education. It was thought that, once this issue was decided, the next thing to do was to spend, spend, spend...

These buoyant expectations were shaken in 1966 when Coleman's final report was released and it was discovered that the home background control variables had "explained" most of the variation between schools with respect to student achievement before anything on the educational inputs list could get a chance! Educationists around the world now had large-scale empirical evidence that their simplistic assumptions about the linkages between educational provision and student achievement needed to be extended to incorporate the substantial influence exerted by the home backgrounds of students.

A little later, the results of the first wave of cross-national studies conducted under the auspices of the International Association for the Evaluation of Educational Achievement (IEA) were released (Husen, 1967). This enormous undertaking, followed later by the even more ambitious survey of six school subjects in twenty-one countries (Walker, 1976), aimed to examine and to disentangle some of the home and school factors that influenced student achievement. These studies generally provided a replication of Coleman's findings concerning the need to recognize the importance of home background factors when considering the outcomes of schooling.

Curiously, the magnitude of the impact of these studies on the world of educational planning had very little to do with their research findings or the final result of the "home versus school effects" debate. Their impact was centred almost entirely on their approach to evaluating educational provision in terms of a capacity to "account for" variation in *educational outcomes*. Until this time, educational planners had been guided in their work by a vision of the perfect school in which "manpower" (administrators, school principals, and teachers) combined with "facilities" (buildings, equipment, and books) to form a well-oiled machine through which students flowed smoothly for a prescribed number of years. The successful planner, within this vision, was able to keep the machine running smoothly by ensuring that supplies of manpower and facilities were appropriate to satisfy student loads. Now, for the first time, educational planners were being challenged by complex questions concerning the manner in which the different elements within this vision could be selected and arranged in order to establish optimal learning conditions. Further, educational planners were being asked to provide firm evidence to show that acceptable levels of student learning would actually take place within the particular configuration of manpower and facilities that had been selected for implementation.

Hard times: planning without direction

It must have been extremely uncomfortable to have been sitting in the chair occupied by the Director of Planning in most Ministries of Education in the mid 1970s. The debate surrounding the studies described above had run its full course by then and in its wake there were very few clear answers provided for educational planners. The "experts" in the educational research field had generally concluded that, instead of answers, we now had a much better idea of the enormous complexities associated with designing and implementing effective educational environments.

To add to the confusion, a growing number of developed and developing countries began to increase the intensity of public interest in educational outcomes by conducting national evaluations of their own education systems. "Accountability" became a catch-cry as educators were pressed to demonstrate that major public investment in education had resulted in measurable gains in student achievement. It was not long before the media started to engage in spirited discussion about matters that were once the hallowed preserve of researchers. The educational planners' aura of technical expertise, for many years the source of their power and influence, was soon diminished as even politicians started to challenge the kinds of planning recommendations that a decade earlier had been accepted meekly by most governments.

Combined with these pressures was the trend for increased decentralization and devolution of decision-making that occurred -- especially in developed countries. This trend left many central planning offices without a *raison d'etre* as many of their activities were increasingly transferred to regional education offices and they commenced to work as collators of plans made at the regional level.

The general dissatisfaction with the direction and goals of educational planning was nearing its zenith in 1976 when the International Institute for Educational Planning organized an "International Seminar on Teaching-Learning Strategies and Educational Planning" (Adams, 1978). The seminar's major conclusions called for educational planners to undertake a major review of their conceptual position and methodological procedures. In particular, it was concluded that educational planners needed to (a) delineate their mission, (b) acknowledge the connection between educational inputs and outputs, (c) employ a rational approach to educational planning for the future instead of a crisis management approach based on "serendipitous guidelines", "inspired solutions", and "ad hoc planning decisions", (d) cease isolating themselves from educational practitioners, (e) recognize that the assumption of clear causal links between the expansion of education and societal development needed further exploration, and (f) establish a solid research support system so that decisions could be made on the basis of evidence rather than speculation.

A new mission for educational planning

The emergence of major economic crises for many countries in the 1980s brought a great change in the settings in which educational systems were required to operate. In many developing countries, especially in Sub Saharan Africa, the economic situation reached a critical point as governments struggled to reduce their national debt by implementing harsh policies that included major cuts in public expenditure and national consumption. The austere measures adopted by many countries to cope with these problems led to a limitation in the resources that were available for education systems and, in some cases, to an undermining of public confidence in the capacity of governments to ensure that there would be productive roles for the young people who graduated from these systems.

Whereas the educational planners of the world were struggling to "delineate their mission" in the late 1970s, the emergence of these difficult economic conditions in the 1980s has established a firm direction for educational planning for the 1990s that requires the preparation of alternative scenarios for improving (or at least maintaining) the quality of education to be presented to governments in association with their implementation costs. That is, decision-makers in the 1990s will demand that proposals for change put forward by educational planners should have a reasonable chance of resulting in improved educational outcomes and/or improved student flows, and that these improvements should be of a magnitude that can be defended in terms of the costs of making the changes.

This new direction for educational planning is likely to extend well into the 1990s and will present many new challenges. In particular, it will require the establishment of a clear conceptual framework that elaborates the linkages between educational information and the quality of education. It will also require the development of sound techniques for measuring, testing, and costing the conditions and provisions that are likely to result in the occurrence of beneficial change. Success in these two areas is essential if educational planners are to break free from an over-reliance on short term crisis management models, and instead develop long-term planning strategies that will allow the transition of education systems from the present to the future to proceed in an orderly fashion based on informed decisions.

Hallak (1989) has pointed out that this kind of evolution in educational planning needs to be fostered by a repositioning of the planners work so that it is "closer to the action". He noted that to achieve this, educational planners would have to become *more pragmatic* -- by taking into consideration the "real" educational, social, cultural, financial, and human dimensions that have shaped the development of education systems, and *more operational* -- by working closely with all of the persons responsible for budgets and resource allocation decisions. In moving closer to the action, educational planners will be required to improve their communication with decision makers. In particular, they will need to assist decision-makers operating at all levels of an education system to articulate important policy-related questions, to define the information required to address these questions, and to design the format and scope of the data collections and data analyses that are conducted in order to deliver appropriate information.

These new approaches and interactions will inevitably result in educational planners moving beyond elementary "input only" and "input-output" models of the functioning of education systems in order to focus more intensively on the processes of education. They will also demand (a) an elaboration of the notion of "educational resources" to include information about the most effective ways in which resources may be deployed within an educational environment, and about their "real" costs -- beyond the usual visible expenditures, (b) a determination by educational planners to seek out less costly educational resources with research-proven effectiveness, such as time management in schools and parental attitudes, that in the past have sometimes been overlooked because of their somewhat intangible nature, and (c) a broad view of the purposes of schooling that will call for the development and application of a wide range of valid measures of valued educational outcomes in the cognitive, affective, psychomotor, and aesthetic domains.

Part I
Information requirements and information collection practices

Chapter 2

Different information requirements for different levels of decision-making[1]

Introduction

Educational planners in most countries have generally focussed their work on matters concerned with forecasting numbers of students, teachers, and support staff, and predicting the demand for, and location of, the buildings and equipment required by education systems at any one point in time (Levin, 1988). The majority of this work has usually provided detailed information about various educational inputs, but has provided little or no information about teaching-learning processes or educational outcomes. The lack of information in these latter two areas has made it very difficult for educational planners to provide the kind of information that would be suitable for making informed decisions about planning the quality of education. This difficulty has often been exacerbated by a lack of understanding within educational planning agencies that the collection and management of useful information about the quality of education requires an acknowledgement that planning decisions need to be made at various organizational levels of an education system (Tyler 1986).

This chapter explores the types of information that might be employed to guide decisions about the quality of education, and presents some approaches for reporting this information in formats

---

1. This chapter was prepared by Anthony Somerset and Mats Ekholm.

that are appropriate for the various levels at which these decisions are made. The discussion has been illustrated by considering four broad groups of decision-makers in education: parents and teachers, school principals, state or provincial officials, and national officials.

The main decision-making levels in education systems

The education "enterprise" in most countries is aimed at facilitating an individual's cognitive, affective, psychomotor and social learning. The persons at each of the four decision-making levels described above need to monitor these activities in order to obtain information that will guide decisions (on a daily, weekly, monthly, or yearly basis) that will influence the educational experiences of those in their change. The types of decisions at each decision-making level will generally be quite different and therefore the type and format of information required at each level will also often be quite different.

Teachers and parents

Teachers and parents need to gather and share information concerning the nature of the educational behaviours (knowledge, skills and values) that have been taught, the extent to which these have been learned by the child, and the contexts in which the child has demonstrated these behaviours with either competence or difficulty. The information about the student's performance needs to be expressed in a manner which permits a clear agenda for teacher and parent action to be prepared. This agenda can only address effectively the child's learning strengths and weaknesses in situations where teachers and parents both understand, and agree to, the nature of the child's educational needs.

School principals

School principals seldom require information about the educational behaviours of individual children. When this kind of information is required, the principal can consult with the appropriate teacher. However, principals often need to be informed about the progress of learning for each class in the school. Information expressed at the classroom level is more suitable for assisting with decisions concerning the deployment of school resources to ensure that all classes achieve the educational goals that have been accepted by the principal, teachers and parents. In addition, the principal needs to have information on how well the school is performing in respect of "core" educational goals that are valued by other similar schools. Principals can use this information to review the school's goals, set priorities among these goals, and focus a whole-school effort on improving the school's learning environment.

State and provincial officials

State and provincial officials do not require information as detailed as that required by school principals because they are far removed from both the daily operations of schools and the daily responsibilities of parents, teachers and principals. The broader role required of these officials, be they administrators, co-ordinators or supervisors, demands that they should make decisions only after having examined information which is sufficient to establish the existence of problems serious enough, or opportunities great enough, to warrant a considerable commitment of their time and state or provincial resources. The main focus of State and Provincial official's attention will usually be concerned with how to employ planning approaches that will provide large groups of schools with the expertise and resources required to set up and evaluate their educational programmes, and then, guided by the results of the evaluations, to adopt procedures that will improve their effectiveness.

National officials

National officials require less detailed information than do state or provincial officals. These officials do not work with individual children or classes, and they are unlikely to concern themselves with the affairs of an individual school or a small group of schools. Rather, their role is to make broad policy decisions concerning the linkages between the legislated directives of past and present governments, and the plans and resources required to attend to these directives. The decisions that they make are expected to have an impact across whole or large parts of education systems and therefore, because of the conservative inertia of educational institutions and the high costs of initiating system-wide change, a great deal of accurate information about students and schools needs to be collated at the system level. It is particularly important for National officials to be sensitive to long-term trends in their education system's capacity to assist all students to make progress towards achieving a high standard of physical, social and cognitive development. In some circumstances these trends will call for intervention in what is seen as an emerging and widespread inability of students to achieve success in a specific part of the curriculum. In other circumstances, the focus will be on the curriculum itself because it may be seen as being in need of revision and restructuring in order to take account of recent research and/or new social and economic conditions.

Some examples of established information sources

In many countries a great deal of the information required for the various levels of decision-making is already available in the form of large-scale data sets obtained from national and international surveys of educational achievement. Some examples are: the Australian Studies in School Performance Project in Australia (Bourke *et al.*, 1981); the Assessment of Performance Unit (APU) in England (Gipps and Goldstein, 1983); National Assessment of Educational Progress in the United States (NAEP, 1986); the 6th, 9th and 12th Grade Surveys in Indonesia (Jiyono and Suryadi, 1982); the International Association for the Evaluation of Educational Achievement (IEA) surveys in some forty countries (Pelgrum and Warries, 1986).

The data associated with large-scale surveys usually contain useful benchmarks of student performance on at least some of a nation's agreed educational goals. In addition, many of the so-called independent variables used in these surveys provide important descriptive information which may be of use to state and national officials.

It is important to note that care needs to be exercised when employing survey data to ensure that the sample designs have been drawn up and executed in a scientifically valid fashion. Those surveys that neglect to provide a clear description of the target population, the objective procedures used to select the sample, the stratification techniques, the stages and units of multi-stage sampling, the procedures used to minimize the dangers of bias through non-response, the size of the designed and achieved samples, and the magnitude of the sampling errors, should be treated with great caution.

Another important source of information may be found in data gathered as part of a national examination system. These data can be provided at many levels of aggregation, for example, as average school scores and as average scores for groups of schools serving communities with similar socio-economic characteristics.

If neither survey data nor examination data are available, then school systems may be faced with the design of their own performance monitoring procedures. In some countries, a "complete census" approach has been used in order to test students from *all* schools in a state or province. A recent example of this has been the state-wide testing procedures adopted by the State of California in the United States (Staff, 1987). Other countries, such as Australia, have adopted a "light sampling" approach with an emphasis on collecting a small amount of data at regular intervals in order to establish time-series data for the education system as a whole (Mc Gaw et al., 1989).

Adjusting information formats and information delivery to the specific needs of different decision-making levels

Teachers and parents

At this level, there is a need for information that is clearly integrated with the teaching-learning process. Therefore overall test scores, for example, that cover whole subject areas are not very useful. Rather, student performance on highly focussed sub-dimensions are required. In the Mathematics subject area, the sub-dimensions could be estimation, arithmetic, calculations, measurement, etc. In the Science subject area, the sub-dimensions could be the solar system, differences between plants and animals, properties of metals, etc. In the Mother Tongue subject area, the sub-dimensions could be spelling, understanding simple sentences, basic grammar rules, etc. Generally, for any reasonable level of reliability in judging a student's capacity to have mastered a domain associated with a sub-dimension, it would be necessary to have student performance information on at least eight or ten items (Morgan 1979).

19

The teacher will be interested in the pattern of performance as shown by the *profiles* of individual student and class performance across the sub-dimensions. For example, consider a situation where a number of students in the class perform quite well on all but one particular sub-dimension. In this case the teacher will be alerted to the need to reflect upon the factors that have prevented effective learning in one specific area. Some of the factors which might have resulted in this unusual pattern might be: (a) that insufficient class time was allocated to learning the material associated with the sub-dimension; (b) that the students were confused by the way in which the teacher explained the material ; (c) that the textbook devoted insufficient space to the material; (d) that no applied examples or homework was given to consolidate the learning of the material; (e) that the material covered for this sub-dimension was unusually complex relative to the other sub-dimensions; and (f) that the material was presented in a fashion that was not relevant to the students's interests and backgrounds.

School principals

The school principal needs several points of comparison in order to know on which sub-dimensions, and at which grade levels, her/his school is doing well or poorly in comparison with other similar schools and in comparison with all schools in the school district. The first point of comparison would be a relative measure of performance -- focussed on the performance level of her/his school with respect to other schools. The second would be an absolute measure of performance -- aimed at providing an indication of the amount of the intended curriculum that has been mastered by the students.

A *relative measure of performance* could be constructed by comparing school mean scores on the sub-dimensions with other similar schools within the same school district. The term "similar" here refers to other schools serving students from the same kind of socio-economic background, having the same standard of staff and equipment, and teaching the same curriculum. The comparisons between these schools could be carried out using breakdown variables which define important groups of students within schools in terms of gender, ethnicity, year-level, etc. One of the important benefits associated with a relative comparison of schools is that it may be possible to learn from the teaching methods and educational environments of other schools that serve similar communities but are more productive in terms of student learning outcomes.

An absolute measure of performance could be estimated by using pre-set levels of achievement which indicate several broad bands of performance for the whole school. For example, if 75 per cent or more of the students at a particular grade level master the material associated with a specific sub-dimension then the performance for this class level is said to be "good". If the percentage of students mastering the material is between 50 and 75 per cent then this is defined as "moderate", and below 50 per cent is designated as "poor". Each of these three levels of performance would lead to different actions being required of the principal. For example, a poor performance level may require a major redeployment of school resources in order to improve student learning, whereas a good performance level may require the principal to reward the students and teachers by providing encouragement and, perhaps, more concrete incentives such as prizes, outings, etc.

State and provincial officials

These officials are mainly interested in the efficient deployment of state-wide and province-wide resources so that all schools, for which they are responsible, have an opportunity to optimize the quality of their educational environments. In some instances, these resources may consist of staff and equipment, whereas in other instances less tangible resources may consist of information and innovative ideas that improve educational outcomes without requiring substantial financial inputs. An example of a successful deployment of the latter type of resource would be found in situation where teacher-constructed curriculum materials that have been shown to improve learning are shared with other schools as part of a pool of proven teaching aids.

The main task of these officials is to look for patterns of results for broad subject areas, rather than specific sub-dimensions, in order to locate opportunities for the state or province to target resources in a more effective and efficient manner. This process may uncover clusters of schools that have, for example, poor performance in Mother Tongue Language but good performance in Mathematics and Science. The existence of such a cluster should prompt a detailed investigation of the reasons for this discrepany in performance.

21

Perhaps, the existence of the cluster be explained in terms of differences in teacher qualifications, curricular differences, or quality of textbooks, etc.?

Where these important patterns exist in school scores it may be necessary for officials to seek supplementary information from "local" sources concerning the special circumstances of the schools in the cluster. An interesting example of this occured during the 1970s in Indonesia where it was found that the Engligh language scores of students in several schools in Bali were far above the scores that could be expected of the most able students in the country. These results were explained following the discovery that the schools were located close to golf courses frequented by English-speaking tourists, and that after school hours, and at weekends, many of the students spent a great deal of time practising their English conversation skills while working at the golf course.

National officials

The National official's task is to address issues concerning the key indicators to be used in order to judge the performance of the education system as a whole. In the past many countries have employed "coarse" performance indicators concerned with enrolment rates and graduation rates. However, more recently, there has been greater interest in highly specific indicators concerned with such matters as attendance rates, retentivity rates, student achievement levels, and discipline problems. Murnane (1987) notes the emergence of this trend in the United States where, although enrolment data had been collected at the national level from 1867, there were no data collected at the national level to assess what students had learned in school until 100 years later.

The "*circumstances*" of schools always need to be taken into consideration by national officials before making decisions concerning their performance as educational institutions. That is, the output of schools, as measured by the amount of learning experienced by students, should be considered in association with the nature of the student intake and the prevailing social and physical environment within which schools operate. If schools are judged solely by the average achievement scores of their students, then many schools that are doing an extremely effective job, given their circumstances, may be misjudged as being ineffective, and vice versa.

For example consider a school that has overcrowed and inadequate buildings, has very few textbooks, has limited access to cultural experiences for its students because of isolation, and has many students from very poor and illiterate families. It would be extremely unfair to judge this school as performing poorly if it was found that the average literacy scores of its students was slightly below the national average. In fact, after taking account of the school's circumstances, it would probably be considered that the school had performed admirably.

The circumstances of schools may be described in terms of two broad classifications of variables that are sometimes labelled as "malleable" and "non-malleable". The non-malleable variables are those that influence the outcomes of schooling, but are not, in the short term, readily amenable to manipulation by persons responsible for the management of the education system. Some examples of these kinds of variables would be the socio-economic circumstances of students' home backgrounds, the geographical environment of the schools, and the distance of school communities from various cultural facilities. The malleable variables are those that influence the outcomes of schooling and, in the short term, may be manipulated by decision-makers. Some examples of these would be textbook provision, teacher in-service training programmes, homework requirements, school staffing, school curricula, etc.

The national official, being less able to influence the non-malleable variables, would most likely be interested in the following two questions: What are the differences between schools in terms of their output, after takining into account school circumstances as measured by the non-malleable variables? Which of the malleable variables arc most influential in assisting schools to become effective? One approach to providing answers to these two questions would be to employ regression analysis to create a measure of school output which has been statistically adjusted for the circumstances of the school, as measured by the non-malleable variables. It should be noted here that the calculation of adjusted scores requires a great deal of care with respect to using data aggregated to the school level. (Keeves and Sellin, 1988.)

This adjusted output measure would be equal to the school residual score calculated by subtracting the "expected" achievement score, obtained from the regression analysis, from the "actual" mean achievement score. a large positive residual score would indicate that a school was performing effectively because it was doing "better than expected" after taking account of the non-maleable variables. Similarly, a large negative residual score would mean that a school was performing ineffectively because it was doing "worse than expected" after taking account of the non-malleable variables. Following these analyses, a sample of very effective schools could then be compared with a sample of very ineffective schools in terms of of their differences with respect to the malleable variables.

In most educational settings the differences between the two groups of schools will probably be associated with a network of interrelated malleable variables. These would need to be grouped according to the different actions that are needed to be taken at the national level. Each action would then need to be costed in financial and administrative terms. When all actions are grouped and costed, they may be presented for further consideration by decision-makers in order to ensure that actions selected for implementation are manageable within a country's economic, cultural and political situation. For example, some actions which involve large expenditures may need to be deferred until better economic conditions prevail, while other actions, which focus on complex ethnic and cultural issues, may require lengthy preliminary negotiations with community leaders before implemenation commences.

Some examples of the use of information to guide decisions concerning the quality of education

Example 1: The improvement of the curriculum through the use of needs assessment surveys

Much important work, usually unpublished, takes place in many national curriculum development centers and units in the world. In order to arrive at the content of a subject area for any one stage of schooling, planners in curriculum centers can conduct "needs assessment surveys". In general terms, there are three main types of needs that are examined by these surveys: the employers' needs of those leaving school and entering the labour market; the needs of the individual to become a good citizen and to be able to develop personal skills; and the needs of the next level of education should the child decide to proceed to that next level.

A needs assessment survey requires the collection of information about the levels of student knowledge, skills and values associated with each of the three sets of needs. The employers needs may be established by conducting a survey using a probability sample of employers in the various domains of work (e.g. agriculture, industry, commerce, the military, etc.), and asking them the extent to which they want to have their employees acquire each of the major educational objectives in the curriculum. At the same time, employers can inform the researchers of other knowledge, skills, and values which they would like the schools to provide. Since national economies are constantly changing, the types of general knowledge, skills and values needed by employers will also change over time and therefore this kind of information must be collected at regular intervals.

It is only the general areas of knowledge, skills and values which can be assessed in this manner because some very specific knowledge and skills are soon out of date. Employers can also be asked to speculate on the general knowledge, skills and values which will be required by those entering their enterprises in five years time. The employers' ratings of "current" and "future" needs can be compared with their assessment of the knowledge, skills, and values currently possessed by their own workforce. These comparisons can be very useful for establishing where the schools are either "overproducing" or "underproducing", and then this information may be used to review the structure of the curriculum.

A needs assessment survey in the area of developing personally and developing as a good citizen can be conducted in a similar way. But, in this case the respondents would be either citizens in general or specific groups within the society. The main aim of such an exercise would be to identify how the society was changing in areas that required different roles to be undertaken by its citizens. For example, in countries where there has been a major swing towards democratic models of government, the citizens will need to acquire sufficient knowledge and skills to be able to participate more effectively in a new political environment.

The third need is for the levels of knowledge required for entry to the next stage of education. Again a survey is conducted on the receiving teachers to assess this. When all of this work is completed, the levels of importance attached to the various parts of the existing curriculum can be gauged and necessary revisions undertaken. There may well be other forces to be taken into account when determining educational objectives. These may include changes in the subject matter itself, parents wishes, students wishes at the higher level of schooling, political changes, pedagogical changes (for example, moving from a tripatite system of education with different curricula to a comprehensive system of education with one curriculum for all), etc. What is important is that information is collected in a systematic way to form a sound basis from which the curriculum decision makers can take their decisions.

The curriculum developers can then develop curriculum blue-prints for the textbooks and materials to be produced, write the materials, revise them, and eventually implement them across the system.

After the changes have settled down in a system, the curriculum center will either assess achievement in various parts of the curriculum or have the research unit of the ministry do it for them. This is usually done by means of a survey and the results would be presented in a similar fashion as was described above. They show those parts of the curriculum being well achieved, averagely achieved, and poorly achieved in the country as a whole, in the different provinces for urban and rural children separately, for boys and girls separately and so on. This allows further revisions to be made to the curriculum to overcome the weak points in the system.

Example 2: The use of examination "backwash effects" to improve teaching and classroom assessment

Most educational systems in the world still have national examinations. Some have continuous assessment and some have school-based examinations moderated by a team of moderators. Examinations determine the future of children and teachers are typically judged within their communities on how well their students do in the examinations. Teachers, therefore, put great emphasis on what they expect the content of the examinations to be.

In many but by no means all systems of education, the national curriculum center hands the blueprint of the curriculum for any one subject or set of subjects to the examinations center and this center ensures that the examinations produced are a true reflection of that which was to have been learned. Even where the curriculum blueprints are handed over, the problem of the quality of examinations remains. There is rarely sufficient time in the examinations to assess all which should have been learned. Different knowledge, skills and values require different assessment techniques: writing, speaking a foreign language, undertaking scientific experiments, comprehension of a mathematical principle, etc. Very often, however, there is considerable disjunction because the range of competencies tested by the terminating examination may be much narrower than the range the country attempts to develop through its curricula, its textbooks, and its teacher education programmes.

There are two main reasons why this happens. In some cases, the content of the examination reflects the needs of the recruiting institutions, rather than the curriculum which the pupils should have been taught. This is especially common with examinations given at the end of secondary schooling and govern access to the universities. In a number of countries, university entrance examinations are set mainly or entirely by university staff, with the consequence that the questions are a better reflection of the requirements of first-year university courses than of final-year secondary courses. In England and Wales, the fact that the universities base selection decisions on just three subjects means that the majority of upper-secondary pupils specialise narrowly, in three subjects only, during their final two years at school. It is widely recognised that more broadly-based courses would be educationally advantageous, but few pupils are willing to undertake them because of the risk that their chances of gaining a university place might be jeopardised.

In a number of developing countries a more important reason for disjunction is that examination centres rarely have access to the considerable resources of money, time, and human skill that are needed to prepare question papers which match curriculum goals. In consequence, the examinations tend to be heavily loaded with questions that can be produced quickly and easily.

These kinds of examinations, for the most part, are composed of straightforward recall questions, which ask the candidate simply to reproduce learned material directly from memory, without reconstructing it or using it in any way. By contrast, questions testing more complex cognitive processes -- which require experience, ingenuity and time to prepare -- tend to be uncommon, or even absent from these examinations altogether. Such questions include those which test pupils' ability to apply what they have learned to new situations, or which require them to show that they understand how facts link to each other, in meaningful patterns of cause and effect. These "higher order" questions focus on thinking skills, such as the ability to interpret and assimilate new information; the ability to develop a logical sequence of steps to solve a problem or reach a decision; the ability to produce imaginative or creative work that is expressive of the unique character of the learner. The development of these more complex, and more useful, competencies has, of course, been a major purpose of recent curriculum and teacher education intiatives in many countries. But unless the examination systems are included in these reforms, their *"backwash effects"* on classroom practice, can place the efforts of curriculum developers and teacher educators in severe jeopardy.

The impact of a major public examination on what teachers do is strongest in the two years preceding that examination. However, in systems where the examination has critical consequences for life chances, the backwash effects often penetrate right down through the school system. In one developing country, for example, where the university entrance examination is entirely in multiple-choice format, many primary school teachers rely heavily on multiple-choice questions for their class tests, even in the infant grades. By Grade 7 or 8, the format of the class test often mirrors closely the format of the university entrance examination.

In many countries, much more effort needs to be made to ensure that the examinations are of the highest possible quality. Apart from the psychometric qualities of validity and reliability, the following three criteria are suggested for judging the quality of examinations.

- *Active thinking.* Testing only recall information is to be avoided. Active ideas are held in the mind as pictures in which elements are linked to each other in patterns. Knowledge-based questions should test understanding of these patterns. Such questions should be concerned with causes, consequences, and reasons; with relationships, trends, and general ideas. In other words with *understanding.* The assimilation of the knowledge is a characteristic of active thinking. Examinations in some subject areas should include a number of data-based questions requiring students to read and interpret new information. Examinations should also include questions testing the *application of knowledge* to new situations including drawing inferences, making predictions, or solving problems. There is always the problem that what is new to one student may not be new to another but, in general, it is possible to construct questions which are known not be in the major textbooks that have been used. The above points have been well known since Bloom's "Taxonomy of Educational Objectives" (Bloom et al, 1956) appeared but surprisingly are often ignored.

• *Equity*. The examination should, to the maximum extent possible, be fair to all groups: to girls, to students living in rural areas, particularly in remote parts of the country, and to those from less-privileged socioeconomic backgrounds. Biases in individual questions are often unavoidable (especially in questions which are experience-based). However the question setters should attempt to ensure that, over the examination as a whole, these biases counterbalance each other as much as possible. This is, however, no easy task. The performance of students in the remote and less privileged schools is nearly always adversely affected by the quality of the education they receive and therefore it is important to ensure that avoidable biases in examination questions do not compound their disadvantage.

• *Open-ended questions*. Even when there is evidence to indicate that, from an assessment point of view, the examination of open-ended questions does not provide additional information for prediction purposes it is nevertheless desirable to include open-ended items simply to ensure that teachers do not only use multiple choice items. It must also be remembered that it is impossible to assess students' ability to develop a logical argument, to defend a point of view, to write essays and the like with multiple choice items.

Example 3: The use of examination results for monitoring the performance of schools and school districts

While examination results are often known at all of the decision-making levels described earlier in this chapter, they are rarely used for monitoring the changing performance of individual schools and districts. This occurs because there is usually no link between the examinations center in a country and those responsible for monitoring the quality of education in the system as a whole.

Schools and districts (especially rural districts) often change their levels of achievement over a period of five years. It is perfectly possible to trace the differing achievement profiles of individual schools and districts and provinces in ways similar to those described earlier in this chapter. The profiles will not be as detailed because typically item results are not used. It is total scores which are used. But the rough estimates provided by exams will be sufficient to judge marked differences over time in terms of the rank order of schools or districts. Where the exams are of a multiple-choice kind then item data can be aggregated in different ways to provide the required profiles. If a sufficient number (about 20 percent) of the items are held common from one year's examinations to the next then a scaling exercise can be undertaken to yield comparable values. This all assumes that item data are recorded. Even though the necessity for recording item data has been well-known in examination centers for a long time, there are still instances of only total scores being recorded.

For examination results to be used at each of the levels it is, of course, incumbent on the examinations center to take the trouble to rank schools, districts, and provinces and feed the information to the appropriate units, education officers, inspectors and advisors. Until this is done, examination data are not being fully used. Perhaps this is a case for top Ministry officials being aware of how such data can be used and then ensuring that the data are produced. The Kenya Certificate of Primary Education Examination provides a particularly interesting example of a well adapted and useful feedback system (see Somerset, 1987).

Example 4:   The use of information from well-designed
research studies to improve teacher education

Information on effective teaching practices needs to be incorporated in teacher education programmes in every country. In ministries of education the Research and Development Center as well as the Department of Teacher Education often conduct studies to identify the "average" teaching practices in their nation's schools as well as those practices which are particularly conducive to good student learning. In the 1980s, several countries combined in an international study with similar aims (Anderson *et al*, 1989). All of these studies have produced results which are of interest. These include poor questioning techniques, few examples used by teachers which are not in the textbooks, poor teacher subject matter knowledge, insufficient use of feedback and correctives, poor structuring and the like. It is obvious that such results have direct implications for the modification (in terms of shifting emphasis) of various components of pre-service and in-service teacher training programmes. However, it seems to take several years for such findings to be incorporated into teachers education programmes. One problem is that the communication of such results is slow and apparently, ineffective.

Good teaching has often been characterized as being like an elephant -- easy to recognize but difficult to describe. Research work in the area is not easy and there have been many poor studies. But, the quality of such research studies is improving. More and more small experimental studies are needed, and the research skills among the researchers working in this area need to be improved. Much can be done at the district and provincial levels in terms of replicated experimental studies which are brought together at the national level. In some countries the departments of teacher education in ministries of education are in charge of the teacher training colleges and the members of these departments spend time as principals of the teacher training colleges. One would expect that this situation would result in the implementation of new research findings being a relatively simple and rapid process but, sadly, even in these countries the rate of implementing new and effective ideas about teaching is extremely slow.

Conclusion

This chapter commenced with a review of the four main decision-making levels that operate in most education systems. It was argued that each of these levels -- teacher/parent, school principal, state/provincial official, national official -- required different kinds of data to be presented at different levels of aggregation. Some established sources for obtaining appropriate information were then discussed in association with some examples of the type of information that is required at each decision-making level. It was emphasized that, in order for information to be employed in educational planning, the format and delivery of the information had to be adjusted to the specific needs of the different decision-making levels. The chapter concluded with a discussion of the ways in which the collection of information associated with curriculum design, examinations, and effective teaching may be used to improve the quality of education and also discussed some strategies for school improvement.

It is important to note that in order to address the information needs of decision-makers in education systems there needs to be effective procedures for the dissemination of information both vertically and horizontally within educational systems. For example, there needs to be a mechanism in each country by which good practices initiated by schools and felt needs expressed by schools are passed "up the education system" and are seen to be dealt with. Similarly, communication "down the education system" needs to be attended to -- with special emphasis being given to matching the format of information to the communication styles of practitioners.

The horizontal dissemination of information, particularly at the national level, among the various units involved in planning education systems also presents problems for many education systems. There are numerous examples of examinations centres not accepting the curriculum blueprint for the construction of examinations, examples of important research on effective teaching not being communicated to planning and teacher training units, and examples of the separation of "long term" and "short term" (often called "strategic") planning units. Perhaps the most widespread example of difficulties in this area occurs when research units operate independently from all major administrative units with the inevitable result that potentially important research findings are communicated in technical language that is impenetrable for the non-research-trained heads of other units that are responsible for formulating policy.

In summary, there needs to be a complete rethink of the modes of communication, both vertically and horizontally, within educational administrations. The work involved in this represents a major undertaking -- particularly when many of the "solutions" to problems are likely to be culture specific. In the first instance, the most effective point of attack on the area would be for international agencies to take up this challenge by initiating some case study research on several education systems in different cultures that have confronted, and found solutions to, information dissemination problems. The reports of these studies could be shared among countries experiencing similar problems and used as stimulus materials for training programmes in this area.

Chapter 3

Current practices, problems, and issues associated with the collection and use of information[1]

Introduction

The aim of this chapter is to describe the efforts that were being exerted at the end of the 1980s in order to plan the quality of education. In particular, it will focus on the use of information at the various decision-making levels of education systems to assist educational planners and decision-makers in their work. There is a great deal of variety within and between education systems with respect to the ways in which information is requested, collected and used. These different approaches are often influenced to a large extent by the degree to which an education system is centralized or decentralized in its decision-making procedures, and also by whether appropriate "machinery" exists for the purposes of data collection.

The chapter is divided into two parts. The first part presents brief descriptions of the current situation in terms of a shift in emphasis from quantity to quality considerations in education, the data currently collected in many countries, and the stages through which countries usually progress in their efforts to collect and analyze data. The second part is focussed on the major problems and

---

1. This chapter was prepared by Arfah Aziz, Boediono, Kiran Dhingra, Viola Espinola, Stephen Heyneman, Lars Mählck and Kilemi Mwiria.

issues associated with the kinds of data collections that are required for planning the quality of education.

In summary, there are two common features that can be identified in the educational information systems that have been developed by many countries. First, there is a gap between the data collected, which mainly concentrate on student enrolment, the number of teachers, and school buildings, and those data needed to plan improvements in the quality of education. Second, most countries do not collect qualitative data about school processes and students' outcomes and are therefore unable to explore the "linkages" between educational inputs, processes, and outputs.

In the following discussion some examples of current practices in this area have been presented. This discussion has been based on an analysis of the "Area Study Papers" and "Theme Papers" (see References Section) that were presented at the 1989 International Workshop on Issues and Practices in Planning the Quality of Education that was coordinated by the International Institute for Educational Planning.

A concern about the content and utility of established educational information systems

In the phase following the enrolment of most of an age-cohort in school, one usually notices a shift in Governments' interest in education from quantity considerations to those of quality. For example, from 1975 Malaysia concentrated efforts on quantitative projects in order to ensure that all children would have a place in the school system. By contrast, since the 1980s, increasing attention has been given to improving the quality of education in the schools. Because of this shift, the educational information system which had been designated to collect data to describe the structure and management of the education in Malaysia, was redesigned in order to collect more data on the achievement levels of the students, on teacher effectiveness, and on the utilization of resources.

In the Arab countries, there was a great expansion of educational services during the 1970s and 1980s that was followed by a growing concern for the quality of the education that was being offered. The predominance of quantitative expansion over qualitative improvement led to deficiencies in the preparation of teachers, poor teaching methods and a low quality of school books and teaching aids. The administrative and information systems, originally designed to meet expansion needs, were shown to be mostly inappropriate for the new efforts aimed at improving the quality of education.

Significant progress has been made in several Latin American countries to expand education, and today the region generally surpasses the 80 percent average enrolment that existed during the 1970s. Data collection and processing facilitated this process by exposing a major problem concerned with grade repetition. It was suddenly recognized that there was a strong need to improve school quality in order to reduce this source of resource wastage. The early educational information systems could not produce, in a systematic way, the body of information relevant for this kind of decision-making, and therefore newer approaches will be required to address this need.

In the countries mentioned above the key problem has been a lack of basic data that can be used to guide decisions concerning the quality of education. However, even in countries that do collect appropriate data, there is often a tendency to structure the data analyses and reporting of findings in a manner that is appropriate only for national level officials. These kinds of educational information systems offer very little that is of practical use to school and district level education managers -- specially those operating in decentralized education systems.

The irrelevance of established national information systems to the local planner was felt in Hungary when the 1985 Education Act promoted decentralization and autonomy and gave the responsibility of quality improvement to teachers and local initiatives. This has also been the case in India where there has emerged a movement towards decentralisation and looking at ways to provide management information to block and district education officers. It is interesting to note that while the educational policy declaration of 1986 in India emphasized an improvement in quality as the major goal for elementary education, the planners at the national and state levels appeared to be not very eager to collect, through the national information system, the kinds of data demanded by local education authorities for their planning and management purposes.

It is important to note that to achieve an improvement in the quality of education requires the direct participation of school and district level decision-makers. These people often have a better feeling for the problems that face schools than do national level officials, and their support and assistance is required in order to collect information that is likely to address these problems. In some countries, basic statistics were provided at all decision-making levels concerning quantitative baseline information on enrolments, staffing, school buildings, etc. However, there were very few attempts to gather information about educational outcomes and educational processes and then provide this information in a meaningful form to school and district level decision-makers.

In the very few examples where administrators at the local level were involved in the collection and use of information about the quality of education, there was a perception that data collections of this type were too expensive and that they were not effective because the local level administrators lacked adequate technical training. This situation was well-illustrated in Sweden during the 1980's when the Country Boards of Education embarked upon systematic reviews of their schools and in so doing collected a great deal of important qualitative information. The use of this information to guide major planning decisions occurred on very few occasions because the local level administrators did not know how to interpret the results of the data analyses. The Ministry of Education in Sweden has taken action to remedy this problem by setting up training programmes in this area for school principals and staff responsible for school management.

Current practices in data collections: the general trends

From the above discussion it is clear that, for educational information systems to contribute to an improvement in the quality of education, there needs to be a great deal of thought put into deciding (a) what information should be collected, and (b) how this information should be communicated to the various decision-making levels of an education system. In the following discussion a cross-national review of the types of data that are collected has been presented in association with some comment about the extent to which these data have been used to improve the quality of education.

The types of data collected in some forty countries, both developed and developing, were examined in order to highlight the general trends in this area. It is these *general trends* that have been presented rather than specific approaches for each of the countries.

The reader interested in more detailed information for specific countries should refer to the workshop papers mentioned above.

Data collections at the school level

(a) The teachers

Teachers in their daily teaching have mechanisms such as questionaires, homework, classwork, teacher quizzes and the like for obtaining feedback from students on their mastery of the various objectives being taught. In some systems, national standardized tests are used to determine promotion to the next grade in school. But, there are many complaints about such tests not being tailored to the specific curriculum either of the nation as a whole in centralized systems or to each school in decentralized systems. In some countries, such as India, with a policy of automatic promotion (that is, no grade repeating), the internal assessments which were originally used for evaluating each student's profile of achievement have degenerated into annual examinations so that, even with a non-detention policy; there are grade repeaters at every stage of the primary school.

The frequency with which teachers test their students are in several cases very high. In Malaysia and Philippines tests are administered weekly and monthly. In the state of Madya Pradesh (India), students are tested at the end of every unit of study (about once a month), and only if the student masters the unit in question can he or she move to the next unit of study.

The tests administered by teachers are sometimes designed by a specialized agency. This is the case in Colombia where the tests are compulsory for all students, but in reality only the schools use the results. In the Swedish comprehensive school and the academic sections of the upper secondary schools, teachers administer centrally designed tests in core subjects to gauge the level of their class in relation to national averages and to guide them in marking their students. The results in such tests also allow teachers to analyze the performance of their students compared to students in other classes of the same school, and also to the students at that grade level the year before. For most countries this type of feedback on student performance is very rarely provided.

In practice, teachers' assessments of their students have not only a diagnostic and selective function but are also supposed to serve accountability purposes. In most countries the teachers are required to update regularly the achievement record of each student and share this information periodically with the parents and the headteacher. Similarly, in most countries the monitoring of student attendance and discipline is another teacher task to which great importance is attached by the headmaster, the school board, the parent-teacher association and by the teachers themselves. Again, there is a good deal of accountability involved in the collection of attendance data since headmasters often have to report these data monthly to state and/or provincial officials.

What is striking in practically all the educational systems considered is the absence of instruments for teacher self-evaluation: either they are not available or not used. It seems that both diagnostic tests to measure subject mastery and checklists on teaching behaviours (including lesson preparation) would be useful at all stages of education.

(b) The school principals

The school principal has multiple functions and occupies a pivotal position both in managing and stimulating the "internal life" of the school. He or she is above all responsible for the general conditions of learning at the school and, in the case of larger schools, this often means not only taking responsibility for the deployment of the school's human and physical resources but, in some cases, also undertaking a substantial amount of financial management. In an isolated rural primary school, the pedagogical, supervisory, and supportive function exercised by the principal may be particularly important.

Regulations in all countries stipulate that each school should keep a certain number of records on their students, staff, buildings, equipment, and the like. In general, these records and registers are designed primarily to enable the principal to submit periodical reports to higher administrative levels. There is universal usage of a basic registration or admission form containing the characteristics of the student such as sex, age, domicile, and name of parents. In some cases, information on the student's family background and health status are collected at the same time. In Chile, for instance, this information is used by the school principal to decide whether the student should receive some kind of special social assistance (supplies, clothing, school lunch, and the like).

For student attendance and achievement, the school principal often receives individual and class reports from the teachers. He then aggregates these for the whole school. The school principal uses such information for keeping parents informed through individual contacts and collective gatherings at the school assembly at the end of each term. Individual learner cards are supposed to follow the students as they move through the education system. The quality of the information appearing on these cards usually varies widely within a given education system and it is not uncommon that cards go astray when the student changes school. In Malaysia, for instance, where such cards or forms are also designed for the career guidance of the student, it appears that they have not been fully utilized since many teachers were not adequately trained to use them.

In some cases student achievement data are used for deployment of school resources. In many districts in Sweden, the schools now use the results on the centrally designed tests -- administered by the teachers -- in core subjects such as Mathematics and Swedish as a basis for distributing extra resources for supportive teaching to students with learning difficulties.

As a rule, secondary schools have their own recurrent budget whereas in most countries the capital expenditures come under the authority of the central and regional levels. The annual preparation of the recurrent budget (which excludes teacher salaries) constitutes an important occasion for the school head and staff to sum up their needs in terms of such items as textbooks and other teaching material, maintenance of equipment and furniture, and the provision of boarding and school meals. This exercise is not limited to expenditures. In some countries, like Kenya where local financing, through school fees and levies for building and equipment funds is considerable, the appraisal and management of revenues becomes an important task for the school principal.

Data collections at the district level

(a) The District Education Officers

In most countries, the "district" constitutes the second administrative level and is located immediately above the school in the formal hierarchy. This is always true for primary education whereas secondary schools sometimes report to officials at more senior levels at the regional or national levels.

The tasks of the district level officers that are cited in all countries refer to the checking and consolidation of returned forms from primary schools. The District Education Officers watch carefully how student enrolment evolves in their district since politicians tend to pay particular attention to this, and since it is a basic planning element in resource allocation decisions which occasionally leads some schools to boost their enrolment figures. Usually the data forwarded by the district level officers to the provincial level are in the form of district aggregates. In many countries there are little or no further analysis at the district level of the centrally designed data collections. In India, for example, the increased information demands from the centre following the expansion and diversification of the education system (with hardly any growth in district level staffing) has left district officers with little time to monitor the functioning of the schools under their supervision.

The district level is supposed to play an important part in the identification of resource needs (equipment, furniture, school supplies, textbooks, etc.) of primary schools in nearly all countries. This assessment can sometimes be grafted onto the Annual School Forms, as in Kenya and Tanzania, but district officials also use their own forms. In the case of India, the national data collection forms are so irrelevant to the needs of the district level that practically every office has devised its own forms. On the one hand, this approach has the advantages of relevance, accuracy, and promptitude. On the other hand, it does not allow the aggregation of data across districts.

A substantial part of this information relates to staffing, teacher posting, transfers, payscales, etc. In Botswana, the District and Town Councils in charge of the management of primary education, particularly physical inputs, at the district level are a primary source of information on individual teacher assignments to schools.

41

However, there is some overlap of effort here because this information is also collected by Education Officer visits to schools and on the annual school form of the central statistical unit. In fact, each Town Council has a planning office whose staff supplement census data with independent surveys and analysis. This is also the case for Hungary (local councils) and Sweden (communes). Assessment of the training needs of teaching and non-teaching staff is another important function attributed to the District Education Officer in Tanzania. Each district office has a special Academic Officer appointed to work on these tasks and to be responsible for organizing training courses for teachers. The same function exists in neighbouring Kenya but the courses are organized centrally by the Kenya Educational Staff Institute.

In some countries, the District Education Officer or his equivalent within municipalities, etc. are supposed to examine special reports that *primary* schools are obliged to submit several times a year, or monthly. Some of these reports refer to student attendance and achievement, teacher attrition and absenteeism. The little evidence available on what really happens to these school reports comes from India. Investigations revealed that at the block level the monthly student attendance reports were not analyzed at all since the amount of work involved in compiling the data was enormous and exceeded, by far, existing staff resources. Returns on student achievement and teacher absenteeism encountered more or less the same fate mainly because of inadequate reporting. District level staff were of the opinion that the "learner records of evaluation" were filled in routinely with pass marks bearing no relevance to actual learning achieved. The annual national level forms submitted by primary schools had more success since district staff at least compiled and forwarded them -- though sometimes without comparing the data with previous years' information or checking with other available sources.

(b) The inspectorate

Some countries have school inspectors at the district level, and some at the provincial and national levels, or a combination of both. The inspectors have many functions, the most common being supervision and inspection of schools and to assist in in-service training courses for school principals and teachers. While the inspectors are often involved in data collections for levels higher than the district level, their working year is usually concerned with one or more districts and, accordingly, they have been discussed at this stage of the chapter.

Some examples of the involvement of the inspectors in data collection are given for three African countries in the following discussion. In Kenya and Tanzania the inspectorate units of the respective Ministries of Education are responsible for the assessment of teaching and learning in the schools and, more generally, for the development and implementation of the curriculum. In Kenya, the inspectorate works in close collaboration with the Kenya Institute of Education. Inspectors are located at the Ministries' headquarters, at the provincial/zonal and district levels. In each of these countries the inspectors' assessments are not confined to purely pedagogical aspects. In fact, an important part of their work is devoted to general school administrative issues including problems of enrolment, staffing, physical facilities, school supplies, maintenance, etc.

The frequency of visits to schools by inspectors vary both between and within countries. In Kenya and Tanzania inspection takes place periodically "as the need arises". This means that some schools have waited years for a visit. In Botswana, every year the Education Officers make a short visit to each primary school. This is followed up by more in-depth inspections of schools that have been identified as having significant problems. Various instruments designed to be used for a systematic assessment of teaching processes and managerial behaviors have been developed in Botswana. A "Competency Instruction Questionnaire" is used by the inspectors when visiting classes. In 1989, work was completed on the preparation of school management rating scales on the effectiveness of the school principal's leadership with staff, and on the rate of implementation of the Ministry's school programmes.

In all cases, written reports prepared by the inspectors are submitted to the Ministry of Education after each visit. Copies are made available to the school, the District and Town Councils (Botswana) and to the Secretary of the Teachers' Service Commission of the Ministry of Education (Kenya). The utilization of the inspection reports remains a serious problem in all three countries: none of them has as yet developed a method for systematically analyzing the information contained in the inspection reports, and no attempts have been made to relate this information to information about the schools obtained from other sources.

Data collections at the provincial/regional level

The tasks of the provincial authorities are, generally speaking, more similar to those performed by the central administration than those of the district office. Moves towards decentralization that have recently been experienced by many countries have, by and large, been a matter of transferring certain activities from the national level to the provincial level and very little indeed to the local level. Nevertheless, the national level still has the final word in decisions on major investments, salaries to teachers in public and subsidized schools, and curriculum content.

Most countries felt that with more trained staff and data-processing equipment at the provincial level the educational planners could have important responsibilities in promoting the quantitative as well as the qualitative development of schools in their region. The main areas where these extra resources were reported as needed were:

(i)   The assessment of school staffing in terms of the recruitment and distribution of teachers to the schools.
(ii)   The utilization of teaching and non-teaching staff.
(iii)   The preparation and execution of annual budgets.
(iv)   The provision of buildings and equipment.
(v)   The co-ordination of school inspection and supervision.
(vi)   The co-ordination of in-service training programmes.

While practices in terms of provincial level decision-making differ from one one country to another, certain common patterns and problems emerge. For example, regionalization of such functions as curriculum and teaching activities, staff management, planning and statistics, and financial management started in the mid 1980s in countries such as Colombia and Philippines (and to some extent in Chile). These countries have all experienced difficulties with the provincial capacity for processing and analyzing data being very limited, and they therefore depend heavily on analyses made by specialists at the national level.

The education systems in Argentina and Malaysia are still highly centralized and the collection and analysis of data describing students, teachers, and schools are mostly undertaken by the central units of the Ministry. The educational information systems in Kenya and Tanzania are also centralized, but some important analyses of centrally-designed forms are undertaken at the regional level concerning teacher and school characteristics and examination results (Kenya). In Botswana, the main part of the sub-national planning and assessment activities takes place at the district level. In Hungary and Sweden, both centralized countries, work is conducted at the provincial level in terms of data analysis of school forms.

India, by virtue of its size and the fact that it is composed of a federation of states, is very different from all the other countries. Many functions of educational authorities in these states are similar to those at the national level in other countries as regards planning and management. Decisions on educational policy for the country as a whole are taken at the federal level which also decides on the allocation of grants to the states.

Usually the provinces collect, and up-date, more specific information than that contained in the national school census. These relate to teachers, buildings, equipment and teaching materials. In countries with regional planning units a series of indicators are calculated -- sometimes on an annual basis but more often every two to three years -- on not only the availability of buildings and equipment but also on their need for repair, replacement schedules, and degree of utilization. Data are also collected on the availability of textbooks in each school, sometimes globally, and sometimes by subject area. Other data collected include the distance from home to school, travelling time, and transport facilities.

Data collections at the national level

Most standardized data collections in all countries are initiated by the national level units for their own information needs. The following description of such data collection activities is divided into two parts: (a) yearly data collections, and (b) periodic but regular data collections.

(a) Yearly data collections

The cornerstone of yearly data collection is the "school census" or "school form" sent to all educational institutions of a country. Originally, its prime purpose was to describe the education situation in a country at a given point of time, and the results were usually presented in a statistical yearbook and other similar publications. The description usually permitted comparisons of educational provision and participation between different types of school, regions and population groups. The data collected in this way were generally used for controlling and accounting purposes, however by the end of the 1980s the school census had come to be seen as a tool for planning, evaluation, and educational research.

In all countries, the emphasis of the school census or school form has always been on quantitative aspects of educational development (number of students enrolled, stock of teachers, provision of classrooms, expenditures, etc). In several countries the school form is no longer annual. For instance, in Argentina and Botswana, student enrolment is assessed three times a year. The responsibility for the school census is generally located either with the Statistical Office or the Planning Department of the Ministry of Education. In Sweden, it is the "Central Bureau of Statistics" -- a multisectoral agency -- that has the primary responsibility for educational statistics compilation.

The second type of data collection exercise comprises those conducted by the various specialized departments of the Ministries of Education. In most countries, the primary and secondary departments send their own questionnaires to the schools under their control. Teacher departments also have their own questionnaires and, sometimes the national Curriculum Development units send out their own questionnaires. In countries with national examination the central examination unit collects, analyzes, and disseminates information on student achievement.

All national level school forms contain some questions on the characteristics of the school itself. These include: the number of mixed schools, boarding schools, the organization of shifts, provision of special education, school meals, health services, library, sports facilities, and so on. Data collected on teachers typically include:

educational level attained, professional training, professional experience (and/or age), and subject specialization.

The most reported indicator is the percentage of qualified teachers at each stage, usually by sex. It is noteworthy that information on teacher turnover and teacher attendance, (two important variables for planning purposes), is neither collected nor analyzed in many systems.

A second set of teacher characteristics on which data are collected are: current post of responsibility , contract term, family status, and salary scale. Those data figuring in the personal files of the teachers are collected or updated either by the central agency for staff management of all civil servants or, more frequently, by the teacher department of the ministry of education. The annual surveys conducted by the teacher department often contain some of the basic elements collected by the school census but also more specific information.   An example of more specific information is the in-service courses taken by teachers and school principals.

The national school form issued by the Statistical Office or the Planning Department typically collects information on the number of existing buildings and rooms according to purpose (general academic rooms, laboratories), the number of classrooms constructed and repaired during the year. In some cases, the form also includes items on sanitary facilities, recreation spaces and services, and meal facilities. Only in a few countries are data collected on the conditions of the facilities. Equipment and furniture do not, as a rule, appear at all in the annual school census. The relative absence of facilities, equipment and furniture in this general instrument is explained by the existence of much more detailed returns in the form of inventories. In several countries, it is the regional office that collects and uses this information, whereas in others this is done by the central primary and secondary departments in co-operation with the regional office.

Several units at the National Ministry of Education have responsibility for the teaching-learning process in different ways. The Ministry's curriculum department establishes the official curriculum and is typically responsible for monitoring its implementation. Decisions concerning the allocation of teachers and distribution of facilities and equipment involve the central planning unit (and the budget department in cases where the two are separated), the primary, secondary, teacher departments and the regional offices. In short, the central units are responsible for certain conditions that determine the teaching-learning process but they deal very little with what happens in the classroom.

This is also reflected in the various national data collection forms and, in particular, the school census form. Generally speaking, they cover only a few aspects of the teaching-learning process. The indicators typically calculated are: number of part/full-time teachers, average workload (hours teaching per week), student-teacher ratio and number of school shifts per day. Only a few countries systematically collect data on the number of shifts taught by the teachers according to sex, age and experience.

The items contained in the school census are not sufficient for decisions concerning the conditions of learning. That is why the schools and districts are requested to submit separate sheets to indicate their estimated needs of teaching and non-teaching staff for the coming school year (and sometimes for two consecutive years), number of new posts to be created and last, but not least, an estimation of the number of additional instructional hours needed. The only regular assessments on teacher behavior, lesson preparation, modes of instruction are those undertaken by the inspectors. However, as mentioned elsewhere, there are great variations in the number of schools actually visited and inspection reports are not systematically analyzed by the central and regional departments.

The usual student characteristics on which data are collected are sex and age, and elective subjects taken (in secondary education). It is not uncommon that student age is not systematically collected. Some systems also collect information on nationality and race but rarely publish any results from analyses using such variables. Types of fellowships received by secondary students appears in most school censuses. The national level planning department uses student data for calculating a small number of input indicators such as enrolment ratios by sex, by rural/urban origin, class size, and student-teacher ratio.

The basic items on attainment contained in the regular school returns concern student progression, repetition and drop-out. They are used by planners for projections of student enrolment, estimations of the number of teachers required for the coming years and for analysis of the internal efficiency of the educational system. Wastage and retentivity indicators at various levels of the educational system are calculated. Sometimes the school form also asks for further information concerning drop-outs in the form of the proportions of voluntary and systematic drop-out. However, in all countries the causes of drop-out are usually collected through special ad hoc studies.

The results from the end-of-cycle and entrance examinations are practically the only data on student achievement collected regularly by the central level. In most countries this is synonymous with data from external examinations. However, there are a few examples of internal assessments where the students' examination results are based on the results of teacher made tests (Philippines and Sweden) or on a combination of both (Tanzania and in some states of India).

The procedures used in external examinations are fairly similar in most countries. The marking and processing of examination forms is done by the central examination unit of the Ministry of Education. Subject scores are computed and then converted into grades. A print-out is produced which indicates the subject and average marks of all students (and whether they passed or failed) by school and gives a frequency distribution for each school. Copies are sent to schools, districts, and the relevant government departments.

In Kenya, the National Examinations Council provides examination results in terms of percentages obtaining given marks by sex and school type. Schools are also ranked by average achievement. Both types of information are reported back to the district officers and to the schools. Such information may be useful for decisions on resource allocations but hardly for the individual teacher who wants to improve his teaching. Therefore, this body also issues a special newsletter for teachers where common errors made by the students are explained and possible remedial measures advanced.

In Sweden, the National Bureau of Statistics keeps individual computerized registers for all grade 9 leavers (end of compulsory schooling) and for students in upper secondary school. Average marks obtained is one of the key items in these individual files together with students' occupational aspirations. In most countries, however, the planning department of the Ministry of Education does not really collect any information from the examination department (apart from the pass/fail rates they receive anyway). This is often regrettable in view of all the other information on students sitting the examination that is collected at the same time. For example, interesting and important analyses on equity issues could be made by linking home background variables and examination results.

(b) Periodic but regular data collections

The second category of national data collection is surveys undertaken at regular intervals. Depending upon the area(s) covered and the resources required, their periodicity varies from every second to every sixth or seventh year. Such surveys tend to cover a few selected aspects of the educational system, but in more depth. They are generally surveys of samples of schools and not full coverages of all schools in the education system.

The surveys are typically one of the five following types:

(i)   The collection of data (over and above those collected by the regular school census) on teacher characteristics, facilities, equipment, etc.

(ii)   The assessment of the teaching-learning process.

(iii)   Curriculum evaluation studies.

(iv)   The measurement of student achievement in core subjects.

(v)   The evaluation of large-scale reform programmes.

There are obviously elements that are common to some of the categories, but for the purpose of this book it is convenient to treat them separately.

The first category is concerned with the conditions of learning at the school level, in particular as regards buildings, availability and conditions of equipment, sports facilities, transportation and the overall standards of the educational services - including the staffing of schools. Hence, this exercise is similar to the activities undertaken at the regional and local level in countries which have adopted a school mapping/micro-planning system.

The assessment of teaching behaviors, teacher student-interactions, and other aspects of the teaching-learning process are tasks undertaken by researchers, curriculum developers, and inspectors -- but with different foci and methodologies. Procedures that combine characteristics of the three have emerged in some countries. One example is the development of the Teacher Competency Instrument in Botswana which is used at regular intervals by specially trained Education Officers to assess teaching practices in primary education and to identify possible areas of improvement. The Swedish "School Review" of upper secondary schools developed by the central educational authority and regional education boards provides another example. These reviews are conducted every two years on a sample of schools and they examine the working habits of the teachers, their use of different teaching-learning aids, the time utilization of both teachers and students, and so on. The methods of data collection are mainly classroom observations and interviews. Copies of the reports are given to all administrative levels from the school to the specialized departments of the National Board of Education.

The importance of recurrent assessments of students' knowledge, and skills, in selected subject areas has been increasingly recognized by policy-makers, teachers and the public in many countries. The last 15 to 20 years have seen a series of national surveys, sometimes linked to international surveys, on student achievement in both primary and secondary education, in developed as well as developing countries. Some examples of these are given below.

In Chile, students in the 4th and 8th grades in primary were tested several times during the 1980s in core subjects such as Spanish, Mathematics, and the natural and social sciences. In 1988, the students' "emotional develoment" was also assessed. The results revealed that, on average, the students mastered slightly more than 50 percent of the objectives that had been set by the Ministry of Education. The resources that were available for remediation did not permit the launching of specific programmes to improve this situation. In 1989, the French Ministry of Education tested all 4th and 6th graders (about 1.8 million students) in reading, writing and arithmetic. The reason for not doing this survey on a sample basis was precisely that it was designed to help teachers to identify the weaknesses of their individual students and organize remedial teaching. The same operation will be repeated during the coming years.

Another example is India, where the National Council of Educational Research and Training did a sample survey a few years ago in primary education which is also to be repeated during the years to come. The so-called All India Educational Survey tested grade V and VII students in English and Mathematics. In some countries, sixth, ninth, and twelfth grade surveys of achievement have commenced but because of lack of resources, they are not undertaken at regular intervals. In other cases, countries have been able to examine how students' knowledge, skills and attitudes have evolved over a 15-20 year period. Samples in both primary and secondary education have been tested in subjects such as Reading Comprehension, Mathematics, Science and English. England is intending to test several age levels of pupils at regular intervals in several subject areas. The United States, through its National Assessment of Educational Progress is now testing probability samples of students in every state to produce state by state comparisons. In short, there is an increase in the number of countries collecting data describing student achievement levels at regular intervals.

The last category refers to data generated within large-scale reform programmes. An interesting case in point is the New School Project ("Escuela Nueva") in Colombia which was launched to improve quality and school efficiency in basic education. This project has, throughout the years, produced a series of analyses on the functioning of basic education of interest to all levels of planning. Similarly, the implementation of the New Primary School Curriculum Programme in Malaysia gave rise to several important evaluation projects. Information collected ranged from student achievement in the three basic skills of reading, writing and arithmetic, to student profiles in other subjects such as Moral Education, Music, and Art and Craft.

Current practices in data collection: problems and issues

The review of current practices in the collection and use of information at various decision-making levels of education systems made it apparent that there were a number of problems and issues that were common to many countries. In the following discussion a number of these matters have been elaborated in detail and, for some of these, suggestions have been put forward for dealing with the associated difficulties.

Difficulty in deciding which information should be collected

Several countries commented on the lack of agreement and clarity concerning which information should be collected. In some cases different units at the national level wanted different information, but there was a lack of coordination among these units. Indeed, in some cases, each unit collected its own information with a great deal of overlap with respect to data collected by other agencies. This problem will be taken up in a later section of this Chapter. In other cases, there was little rethinking of which new information should be collected and which should be discarded. A typical comment emerged in a paper describing the situation in Hungary: "Nobody can tell us exactly in advance what kind of data should be collected. Consequently, it often occurs that very different and large amounts of data are collected without clear objectives".

In part, problems occur in this area because many planning offices have not thought carefully about linking educational inputs to educational outcomes. That is, they have rarely asked themselves: which inputs affect achievement more than others, given the social background of the intake of students to the school? Decisions concerning which inputs and outputs should be measured requires a knowledge of the research literature on the relative effects of inputs on outputs and also requires educational planners to develop hypotheses about the linkages between these which may operate in a special way within a country. What is clear is that educational planners do want information on the relative effects of input variables but that these linkages are rarely conceptualized or tested.

In many countries there are some *ad hoc* research studies that have attempted to identify, on the basis of these linkages, the more important from the less important variables affecting student achievement in different subject areas. This is a basis for the beginning of a literature review in each country. Unfortunately, the researchers responsible for the *ad hoc* studies often write their reports in such jargon that it is difficult for educational planners, many of whom are not researchers, to penetrate the text.

There is a clear need for national and international agencies to develop appropriate training programmes that will address the shortcomings in this area.

Multiple agencies of data collection

Apart from the need for national planning, data are also collected for purposes of improving specific aspects of the educational process. For example, data are collected concerning the improvement of classroom teaching-learning procedures, try-outs of educational materials in order to assess their suitability for classroom use, tests of curriculum choice and sequencing, and various strategies aimed at improving teacher training programmes. In some situations, data collection is also conducted to identify the needs of special groups of children.

These data may be collected at school or district levels, or by central data collecting agencies, as well as by teacher training colleges, and various sections in the Ministry of Education, such as the curriculum centre, examinations centre, textbook section, supervision and inspection section. Other than these departments, universities, donor agencies, non-governmental organization and privately owned consulting firms are involved in the collection and analysis of education data.

In many cases, some agencies seem to collect this information without realizing or knowing that others are all collecting the same kind of information. There often seems to be a lack of communication between these agencies as to the kind of information to be collected and the purpose for which these data are collected. For example, in Kenya data describing teaching staff (personal characteristics, qualifications, etc.) are collected by the central Bureau of Statistics (CBS) of the Ministry of Planning and Economic Development, the planning and statistics units of the Ministry of Education, the Teachers' Service Commission (TSC), the Inspectorate and the 8.8.4 Bureau (the department responsible for data collection on the newly implemented 8.4.4. System of Education). The same duplication is evident with relation to a good deal of student and school level data. At the student level, data on enrolments are gathered by the CBS, relevant units within the Ministry of Education and the TSC. The same is true of school level data relating to school identification, location, size, type of school (day or boarding, single or mixed sex), the scope of the catchment area, and on the number of teachers available in each school by subject specialization.

In addition to major overlaps, there would also appear to be little integration of what is collected. In Hungary, for instance, there is little integration between the various types of data gathered by different sources mainly because different personnel are involved in the data gathering exercises. This seems also to be the case in Tanzania, India and Indonesia.

Educational planners themselves have not been able to use a lot of the data gathered because the results of the analyses tend to appear long after the data have been collected. For instance in Kenya, the last regular issue of the Ministry of Education was the Annual Report of 1979. Annual Reports for the years 1985-1988 have yet to be published. Even when these data have been analysed, they may not always be easily available to practitioners or researchers outside the top levels of the ministry.

A further problem associated with these annual reporting mechanisms is that many researchers, especially those associated with donor agencies, tend to be cynical concerning the validity of the results of the Ministry of Education data. They note that many of these data are characterized by large margins of error due to inaccurate data gathering and data analysis techniques and very high non-response rates. It is also true that, in some cases, political factors may influence the results eventually published by ministries of education -- especially where the distribution of educational resources is in question.

Thirdly, and related to the above reasons, donor agencies tend to push for their own studies irrespective of what other relevant data may be available. This occurs not only because donor agencies tend to distrustful of studies carried out by ministries of education but also because they may have their own different agenda. Fourthly, ministries of education may find it difficult to use data from university initiated research studies because of their sometimes rather radical overtones, use of (sometimes overly) sophisticated data analysis techniques and academic jargon, or because many of the products consist of case studies not always generalizable to the society as a whole.

Finally integration of ministry data and those from other sources is hampered by a lack of effective research coordinating units. In both Kenya and Tanzania, for instance, a great deal of duplication characterizes the educational research environment. In countries where many basic needs are lacking and in which research could be perceived as an expensive luxury, such duplication is unfortunate. A well planned educational data bank would go a long way to limiting the extent of such duplication.

In this regard the examples of the Latin American Network of Educational Documentation, the Teacher Training and Research Centre, and the South East Asian Bibliographic and Abstracting Service, provide models worth emulating. The Latin American Network integrates most research done by non-governmental organizations in Chile and includes most of the educational research carried out in Latin America. The Teacher Training and Research Centre runs an information network which includes most of the educational research carried out in Chile and other Latin American countries. The two networks also conduct periodic studies which are later published. The South East Asian Centre collects citations of research in the field of education from which selected titles are abstracted to form the basis of state-of-the-art reviews. Following in the footsteps of the Latin American and Asian networks, the Educational Research Network of the Eastern and Southern Africa is now in the process of launching an educational research data bank.

The multiplicity of efforts in this area by various government, non-government, and international agencies is often very wasteful. In many countries there is a need to "take stock" of what data collection activities are being undertaken with a view to rationalizing and streamlining information collection procedures.

Control of and access to data

Both raw and analysed educational data are accessible in varying degrees to different sets of individuals, groups of individuals and institutions directly or indirectly associated with education. These groups include senior Ministry of Education bureaucrats, politicians, donor agencies, Boards of Education and Statistics, Committees or Commissions inquiring into educational systems, national and regional research associations, and to some extent parents, teachers, and students.

Donor agencies operating in developing countries have considerable access to countries' educational data. This is mainly because they tend to insist on understanding specific educational systems before putting their money into given educational programmes. Other than having access to data available in Ministry of Education offices, they also tend to gather their own data through evaluation missions and consulting contracts. It may be difficult for poor third world countries to refuse such agencies access to the data they ask for because many of them badly need the aid such donors are likely to offer.

In the industrialised countries, university researchers have considerable access to data which is considered a "public good" whereas in developing countries, educational data may be considered to be touching on sensitive state matters and may therefore not be made available to researchers. In Malaysia and Indonesia for instance, although educational data relating to ethnicity are gathered, results emanating from the analysis of such data are rarely published. In other parts of the world, particularly Africa, educational data touching on ethnicity are not collected. National and regional research associations in Africa, Asia, and South America have some access to educational data, although their ability to use most of the available data in their respective regions may be limited by their lack of legal status. The point to be made here is that a concern with national security may sometimes make it impossible for government authorities to make some educational data available to all those in need of them.

In both the industrialized and developing countries, parents, teachers and students have the least access to educational data. The differences between the two sets of countries in this regard being more one of degree. Whereas parents, teachers and pupils in the industrialized countries may have some limited access to published material reporting on educational trends, this is hardly the case in most developing countries. The data that are most accessible to these groups are mostly those focussing on examinations because performance in examinations, especially those used for university selection, greatly influence one's chances of upward social mobility. Apart from these examination data, parents, teachers and students generally have limited, or no, access to most of the educational data used for policy-making.

Inadequacies in data collection

In many countries too many data of limited utility are often collected. This is a result of bad planning in which the statisticians or educational planners have either not considered fully the needs of the decision-makers in the education system, or they have over-estimated the capacity of the system to collect, analyse, or properly disseminate information, or they have failed to be sufficiently selective in terms of the data they have requested.

Decision-making needs in many countries are often not analysed in any systematic manner before decisions about the data that should be collected are finalised. This usually results in the collection of data that are redundant or are not useful in decision-making.

Some examples of the collection of these kinds of data are:

- Indicators that do not relate to the decision making process and are therefore redundant. For example, information relating to "use of school library" -- "availability of midday meal" when there is no library or midday meal scheme.

- Continued data collection in programmes that have been discontinued.

- Management systems that are more sophisticated than education decision-making procedures are sometimes set up without considering the readiness of the system to absorb and utilise the data. For example, in education systems where decision-making is still a political or *ad hoc* process, the data collected, however relevant, are often never referred to.

The problem of "Too many data"

The number and kinds of items that an educational information system should include vary according to the capacity of the varying data processing systems. Under-staffed offices and ill-trained personnel are a serious constraint, especially in a data processing unit. Another important consideration is the capacity of the unit to use available technology. To illustrate, a micro-computer at the school permits the planner to obtain as much information as he or she wants, with little constraint from data processing sources. Whereas a micro-computer at the district level means some constraint due to teacher-time available for filling in forms, but takes care of several problems of consolidation and aggregation. Unfortunately, most developing countries are not at the stage where computerisation has reached below the central or provincial levels. These countries have had to simplify problems of data collection and transmission by being extremely selective in their choice and use of indicators. In manual processing systems, the capacities of the school teacher and the local levels to collect, consolidate, and transmit data are likely to remain important issues in planning the amount of data that an education system may collect in an accurate and efficient manner.

Census versus survey sampling for data collection

The collection of data from all schools is an expensive operation. For many indicators data can be collected more effectively and more cheaply through survey sampling. The number of schools required in a sample survey is many fewer than all schools. Indeed, a sample of 150-200 schools will often yield very accurate estimates for a country with thousands of schools.

For a district or province which must look at every school in its jurisdiction in terms of enrolment, lack of space, or a pupil-teacher ratio under a certain level, it is possible to devise a very short questionnaire. This can be processed at the district and/or province level, however for many other variables a sample survey will often be adequate.

Perhaps because analysed data are often late in being presented to the policy-makers, educational planners attempt to compensate for this by demanding annual, or in some cases even quarterly, returns. On the other hand, some countries are reducing the frequency of census data collections. In India, some statistics are now collected only every three or five years. There are several indicators, such as conditions of buildings and availability of hostels, which are rather static unless there are specific building programmes for these purposes. Such data need only to be collected every 3 to 5 years.

There would appear to be an unspoken suspicion, or lack of confidence in data collections based on sampling as compared with a census. This stems partly from a fear of poor sampling that has been undertaken to date in many studies, and partly from concerns that provincial or district disparities will be clouded over if sampling is employed. Serious attention should be given to using survey sampling. Proper training on sampling procedures and a better understanding by educational planners of the sampling procedures now available should help in this regard.

Financing issues

The single most important determinant of data collection policies is the question of who pays for it. By and large, financing for research and management information comes from the Ministry of Education at the central, or in large federal systems, at the state level. Generally, the organization which pays for data collection and analysis determines the nature of the data collected and the forms of analyses conducted. This creates problems of three kinds:

(a) *Lack of diversity in finance.* Because there are many different organizations and institutions with interests in having data collected, it is common practice to require more information without supplying sufficient financial resources. It is common for Ministries of Planning and Finance to require new data for financial planning, and it is common for central authorities to require new data collection efforts on the part of the school or local school district. But it is rare that new resources are provided to cover the additional costs.

(b) *Lack of incentives.* Because financing comes politically from above -- and from a single source -- there are few incentives for schools or school teachers to collect information well. There are few examples of funds being provided to local schools to collect their own information or to analyze information collected previously. In sum, many of the difficulties in generating appropriate utilization of educational quality data can be attributed to inelasticity in the mechanisms by which data collection and analyses are financed.

(c) *Unit costs.* Data are often collected to calculate unit costs (per student, per desk, per laboratory, one day's in-service training, etc.). It is not enough to know that ten more science kits per classroom would be likely to increase science achievement, or that one more day in-service training per year for all teachers would be likely to increase overall achievement. In addition to this information, it is imperative to know the unit costs so that educational planners can calculate the overall investment required in order to introduce major changes into an education system. The unit costs in education are often incorrectly calculated and this is clearly a field where major training initiatives should be mounted.

Perennial gaps in information

Duplication of information is common. So is the prevalence of under-utilized information, inappropriate information, and unanalyzed information. In spite of this, the most serious problem in planning the quality of education is the absence of information on a small number of crucial issues. There continues to be an absence of information on *unit expenditures* -- including the contribution of private fees and voluntary organizations; there is little regular information on *academic achievement,* either for diagnostic or for purposes of system evaluation; there is a total absence of information on the *subject matter knowledge of teachers*; and there is usually no information on *student timing and tracking* -- the time spent in contact with specific curricular objectives and on levels or types of curricular (tracking) options.

These pockets of absent information are serious on a national scale, but they are worse when considered internationally. International studies concerned with comparisons of academic achievement have been plagued by each of the categories of problems identified above. They have suffered from a substantial level of over-expectation and under-funding. In addition, there have been continual difficulties associated with these studies of having a surplus of information on topics which are of questionable use in the aggregate, and a dearth of information on the most critical parts of the educational system -- costs and sources of finance for instance. Like other problems in the current methods of measuring and analyzing problems of educational quality, the means by which international comparisons are conducted will have to be improved in three ways: (i) Duplication will have to be eliminated; (ii) Funding and incentives for appropriate use of data at specific decision-making levels will have to be guaranteed; and (iii) collection mechanisms will have to be regularized.

Conclusion

This chapter has presented an overview of current practices, problems, and issues associated with the collection of information aimed at assisting decision-makers working at various levels of education systems. It was demonstrated that there was a wide variety of approaches both between countries and within countries at the different decision-making levels.

The discussion of problems and issues presented in the second part of this chapter highlighted a need for some internationally coordinated research and training programmes in this area. In terms of "needed research" there is an urgent requirement for research into (a) decisions concerning what information should be collected in order to construct useful educational information systems, (b) the ways in which overlaps and redundancies associated with data collections can be removed, and (c) the techniques that would be appropriate for identifying and addressing important gaps in data collections. In terms of "needed training" it was shown that there are obvious gaps in the skills of educational planners in many countries in terms of basic technical skills required to mount and manage educational information systems that provide useful inputs to decision-making at the various levels of education systems.

In order to attend to these research and training areas it will be important that an internationally coordinated effort be mounted. This approach is required not just because of the scope of the problems that have been identified, but also because many countries working together on these problems will be more likely to lead to the kind of sharing of expertise and experience that is likely to result in a successful and timely resolution of problems for a broad spectrum of developed and developing countries.

Part II
Educational information and the quality of education

Chapter 4

The relationship between educational information, educational management and the quality of education[1]

Introduction

In the academic world we usually approach planning issues by beginning with the notion that good decisions are informed decisions. That is, we tend to view planning questions as mainly technical matters in which the goals are reasonably clear and the information required to tackle the questions is mainly value free. In the area of social policy, this view often results in the initial response to a difficult planning question consisting of a call for more and better information. Such responses generally carry the assumption that there are clear and unambiguous connections between information and the improvement of social conditions.

Unfortunately, in the field of educational planning, these connections are not easy to establish, and they are sometimes subject to alternative interpretations that depend upon the particular research paradigms employed to establish them. Educational planners need to recognize these difficulties and thereby resist the temptation to set up educational information systems in isolation from a sound conceptual

---

1. This chapter was prepared by Henry Levin, Douglas Windham and Zoltan Bathory.

framework that illustrates the linkages between the information that is to be collected and the related actions that are expected to improve the quality of education.

This chapter seeks to explore the linkages between information and the quality of education by commencing with a consideration of the historical context of information's role in the management of education, and then presenting some examples in which educational information is employed systematically in an educational planning context for the purposes of constructing "status indicators" and "action indicators".

Educational information and educational management

The current situation

In both developed and developing nations over the last forty years there has been a steady growth of interest in the creation and expansion of educational information systems designed to provide information that will assist with decisions concerning planning the quality of education. This interest has often been encouraged through the financial contributions of external donors and other international agencies. It has also been encouraged by the intuitively obvious need to measure the costs and effects of education systems which have become a major component of public (and private) budgets and a source for the development of human resources required to support national development. Recent initiatives in this area have encompassed status and needs assessments, the monitoring of progress, and the evaluation of individual, institutional, and systemic capacities.

The nature and degree of success associated with these efforts has generally been country specific. In particular, many educational information systems have been plagued by an excessive focus on aggregated measures of qualitative change. There has also been a tendency for the supply of data to exceed the capacity of decision-makers to use data as an information base for decision-making. Focussing specifically on the issue of education systems designed to improve the quality of education, most countries have experienced fundamental problems associated with a lack of congruence between data availability, information needs, and utilization capacity.

Within the context of individual national priorities and capacities, the development of these information systems has required decisions to be made about the following important matters:

- An operational definition of educational "quality";
- A macro-educational, micro-educational, or multi-level orientation;
- A focus on inputs, process, or outputs;
- The use of a specific conceptual framework to select educational indicators or the acceptance of an ad-hoc system;
- The relative emphasis on data continuity and ease of collection versus the information needs of users; and
- Whether to focus on information requirements for educational policy-making, planning, or practice.

In the four decades since the education information systems movement began its major growth in the United States and Europe, these design issues have usually resulted in an acceptance of the following features: ambiguous or varying definitions of the quality of education, systems with a macro-educational orientation, a focus on inputs, an ad-hoc process for identifying indicators, a lack of consideration for the needs of data-users except for those with requirements for highly aggregated data, and a nearly unanimous inattention to the information needs of educational practice.

While the reasons for this situation are neither complex nor sinister, the effects of these design decisions have been to restrain the capacity of education information systems to assist in the enhancement of the quality of education, however it is defined. In order to better appreciate some of the forces that have shaped these design decisions, it is helpful to consider the historical context of information's role in the management of education systems.

The historical context

(a) Bureaucratic models derived from the "principles of scientific management"

The core principles of what now is regarded as basic management practice were first specified in Frederick Winslow Taylor's 1911 publication, *Principles of scientific management.* Taylor posited four key attributes for the management of any organization or activity:

(i) Intuitive methods of decision making should be replaced by a more scientific method based on observation and analysis;
(ii) Managers should be selected for their positions scientifically be appropriately trained;
(iii) Managers should ensure that work is carried out according to established standards and procedures; and
(iv) Duties should be allocated so that managers assume responsibility for the key tasks of planning, preparation, and supervision.

Taylor did not supply an actual theory of administration, but his four principles became core aspects of many later theories such as "Management by Objectives", and "Program Budgeting Systems" and led directly to the development of modern management information systems. Taylor's first principle, emphasizing as it does a shift from *intuition to inference*, requires for its application a basic set of data from which inference may be derived. Analysts were later to point out that the quality of this information set could be judged in terms of four of its characteristics: relevance, accuracy, timeliness, and understandability (Chapman and Windham, 1986).

Taylor's other three principles -- relating to recruitment and training, operational rules, and allocation of responsibility were incorporated into Max Weber's (1946) description of "bureaucracy" as a pure organizational form. Weber identified three forms of organization based on the nature of authority: charismatic, traditional, and rational-legal. While the first two identify authority as originating in the personality or inherited position of the leader, only the third assumes that authority will be logically derived and legally sanctioned. This third form of organization was what Weber entitled "the bureaucracy". It was characterized by a well-defined hierarchy of authority, functional specialization in work, rules and procedures for dealing with problems and questions of responsibility, impersonal work relationships (in opposition to nepotism and other forms of personal favoritism), and extrinsic rewards based on meritocratic standards of performance.

At present, the only phenomenon more common in educational systems than bureaucratic structures is the criticism of them. Such criticisms often fail to comprehend that bureaucracies originally evolved to promote equal, not arbitrary, treatment. Clients were to be served according to rules and not in terms of their status or influence. This "egalitarian premise" of bureaucracies, however, is often violated by the co-existance of the bureaucracy in a political or cultural environment that pressures for recognition of status and influence and, in the case of education, the fact that the teaching-learning process itself is not sufficiently standardized to allow a set of fixed rules and regulations to meet its highly variable needs.

(b) Political models as "Organized anarchies"

Contemporary with Weber's work, there was the development of political models of decision-making that challenged the principles of scientific management. Herbert Simon (1945) and, later, Simon and James March (1958) attacked the core premise of scientific management by challenging the assumption of rationality in decision-making. March has since led the way (Cohen, March, and Olsen, 1972) in promoting the concept of educational institutions as "organized anarchies" characterized by problematic goals, unclear technologies, and fluid participation by members. As an alternative to the concepts of rationality and efficiency at the core of "scientific management," the political models of educational organization view educational institutions as consisting of coalitions, with the manager serving primarily as a political broker. The coalitions that exist tend to be either structural (related to group or department function) or ideological (focussed by specific desires for organizational change or maintenance).

As these competing perceptions of management have evolved, they have continued to be adapted to the public sector and especially to the field of education. Often this has occurred without proper consideration of the significant differences between private and public sector organizations (Bower, 1977), and of the unique nature of education among public activities (Hanushek, 1986; Klees, 1986; Windham, 1988).

(c) Applied science models based on "Informed intuition"

During the 1980s, the "applied science" model of educational management has become popular (in practice if not with theoreticians). The applied science approach views knowledge as an instrumentality for the manager (Kennedy, 1984). Borrowing from the traditions of both Taylor and Weber, this view asserts that the best information available should be applied to the identification and definition of problems and then to selecting a treatment based on accepted current practices.

In application, the applied science model often is merged with what Sergiovanni et al. (1987) describe as "reflective practice." This model posits that professional decision-makers rely heavily on informed intuition as they create new knowledge and that such intuition is informed by theoretical knowledge and an appreciation of the management environment. This model incorporates both the examples of "self-evident evidence" and of "practitioner knowledge" discussed later in this chapter.

The model also implies that there exists some reasonable basis for linking information with action, and that appropriate linkages emerge both through the decision-maker's continuing participation and experience in the field and through his/her interactions with skilled practitioners. In the following section of this chapter several views of the nature of these linkages have been explored.

The relationships between educational information and the quality of education

A central theme of this book is the notion that educational planners operating at different levels of an education system require different kinds of information in order to guide their decisions concerning planning the quality of education. This theme immediately raises the question of *how* information and the quality of education are related. Surely, one would be hard-pressed to prove that the mere provision of more and better educational information will improve the quality of education. At best, the availability of appropriate information is a necessary condition for improvement, not a sufficient one. In order to identify and collect the kind of information that will be useful for raising the quality of education, one must first ask under what conditions will educational information improve quality.

It is useful to begin with an idealized example in order to explore the role of information in affecting quality. Imagine a hypothetical decision-maker at the school district level who is committed to the goal of raising the mathematics achievement of students. From her knowledge of the determinants of mathematics achievement, she has an excellent understanding of the different inputs that can be used to improve mathematics knowledge and skills. As a first step, she gathers information on the current level of each of these inputs, the most recent research on the effects of additional increments of each input on mathematics achievement, and the relative cost of each input. This information, which is both readily available and accurate, enables her to deduce the present levels of each input as well as the comparative cost-effectiveness of different strategies for improving mathematics learning. From an educational planner's perspective, she can now decide whether to reduce those inputs that are least cost-effective and reallocate the savings to those that are most cost-effective, and then allocate any increase in her budget in a way that will maximize the gains in mathematics achievement.

In this idealized example, the availability of educational information that was related to a decision-making objective made it possible to improve educational quality by improving the educational environment of students in a manner that could reasonably be expected to result in increased levels of mathematics achievement. However, there were a number of major assumptions contained within the example. First, it was assumed that the objective was clear (raising mathematics achievement), and that the decision-maker had an incentive to focus on that objective. Second, it was assumed that the decision-maker had acquired a good understanding of the conceptual framework required to interpret and use information about inputs, outputs, and costs. Third, it was assumed that appropriate information on levels of inputs and costs and the effects of changing these levels was available. Finally, it was assumed that the decision-maker could change input levels, without being constrained, for example, by political factors.

The four assumptions that underpin the linkages between educational information and the quality of education in the hypothetical example presented above must *all* be satisfied if educational information is to play a central role in improving the quality of education. That is, the availability of information by itself is unlikely to guarantee an improvement in quality.

In the following discussion, two approaches to the use of educational information to improve the quality of education have been presented. These approaches are characterized by different sets of assumptions concerning the linkages between information and quality. The first approach considers how educational information could serve to promote increased accountability by providing indicators of perceived quality for the whole of an educational system and for particular parts of that system. The second approach examines how information about an education system could be used to guide decisions aimed at improving the quality of education.

Educational information as "Status indicators"

Every society has certain explicit or implicit measures or status indicators of educational quality (Murnane, 1987). In general, these indicators can be divided into three classes: educational inputs, educational outputs, and educational processes. Inputs include financial measures, physical measures, and manpower measures associated with the resources that are provided for students at each educational level. Financial measures are generally summarized by educational expenditures per student. Physical measures include the age, condition, and comprehensiveness of such facilities as classrooms, laboratories, and libraries and the provision and use of international materials and equipment. Manpower or human resource measures include the number of personnel of different types, often expressed as ratios in relation to student numbers at each level. They also include background information about these personnel such as educational qualifications, experience, and perhaps knowledge competencies and attitudes.

Educational outputs refer to the consequences of the educational process as reflected in measures such as the levels of knowledge, skills and values acquired by students, and the later careers of graduating students in terms of, for example, educational accomplishments assessed by the proportion of students participating in post-secondary education.

Educational processes refer to the interaction between students and the personnel, the curriculum, the course requirements and offerings, and the organization of the educational environment as well as co-curricular and extra-curricular activities. This interaction will be influenced by various other mediating factors such as levels of parental and community support and encouragement.

There is abundant empirical evidence to demonstrate that these inputs, outputs, and processes are related in the sense that the use of different inputs and processes should affect the outputs of the educational system. But, while we acknowledge that these important causal linkages exist, it is important to recognize that the availability of information describing these three areas is no guarantee that we will be able to improve the quality of education. That is, the availability of information by itself often restricts our knowledge of the education system to an assessment of current status.

One might view educational indicators as comparable to health status indicators in terms of their relation to quality. A medical examination with x-rays and laboratory tests may reveal that one has a specific health status that is sub-optimal; it may even identify the ailment. But, it does not in itself set out a strategy or mechanism for getting well. In response to the diagnosis it is often necessary to have resources with which to effect a cure. Even with resources, one must chose a "technology" which one believes will provide a cure. Clearly that technology will differ depending upon whether one believes that health status is derived through nutrition and exercise, herbalism, spiritualism, acupuncture, homeopathy, or western medicine with its penchant for prescription drugs and surgery. The point here is that the presence of even an elaborate system of indicators for either health or education does not assure the existence or the use of a strategy that will raise quality.

For this reason, educational status indicators constitute a passive information system rather than one that leads directly to a strategy for raising the quality of education. At best, one might use the information generated by such a system to develop hypotheses that may be explored for their utility in improving the quality of education. The testing of such hypotheses might even draw upon some of the input and process measures in explaining outcomes. But, even this extension of a system of educational status indicators requires some assumptions about the connections between the use of information and strategies to raise quality. Educational status indicators are, therefore, best used for their heuristic value rather than their deterministic implications for improving quality.

Educational information as "Action indicators"

In order for information to be used to improve the quality of education through better decision-making, there must exist a sound theoretical or conceptual framework that ties decisions that use this information to higher quality. Such theories need to go far beyond description to the realm of prescriptive or predictive relations that will guide the adoption of strategic actions. That is, one needs to tie the various policies, processes, and inputs to the outputs that are being produced. Only in this way can one convert information into sound strategies for raising the quality of education.

(a) Building on educational production functions

In a situation where the goals of an education system are sufficiently clear with respect to desirable educational achievement outcomes, it is usually possible to employ an educational production function approach to establish empirically the linkages between the levels of educational inputs and processes that are associated with improved educational outcomes. If the prices of these inputs and processes are known, and the inputs are manipulable with few political or technical constraints, the educational planner could scrutinize the information on inputs and outputs and suggest policies for improving quality that would be cost-effective in the sense that the effects of each of the inputs and processes on output could be considered in association with their cost (Levin 1983).

Unfortunately, more than twenty-five years of work on educational production functions has revealed just how elusive these relations can be (Hanushek, 1986). They seem to vary from study to study and to depend upon the sample of schools, the specification and measures of inputs, and the techniques of estimation (Hanushek, 1986; Heyneman and Loxley, 1983). This is not to argue that such relations do not exist, but that they are difficult to measure and use as a basis for a strategy that will improve quality in a predictable manner.

In part, the problem seems to be that many measures of inputs and processes are extremely difficult to measure in a reliable and valid fashion. For example, an input measure of "access to school library facilities" might be made by calculating the number of library books that are available per student. However, this measure would not address the issue of precisely how many books, of which kind, of what level of excellence, etc. are being used by each student. Some schools with very large libraries may have low levels of library access because of a very poor selection of books, or they may have restrictive borrowing rules, or there may be little encouragement given to students to use the library facilities. Similarly, a range of "teacher behaviour" variables may be measured on the basis of observations gathered for a few hours of teaching. These observations may be unreliable and/or invalid because the few hours selected for measurement may not be representative of the general pattern of the teacher's behaviour.

Despite the lack of a solid knowledge base that would permit the use of educational information to set out strategies for manipulating inputs and processes in order to improve educational outcomes, the production function framework is the dominant conceptual one for building educational information systems. While experience with this approach has yielded some guidelines for consideration (Lockheed and Verspoor, 1989), they do not always provide findings that permit a straightforward translation of available information into precise strategies for improving educational quality. At best, they suggest directions that are likely to yield better results than other directions. This means that even at central levels the use of formal theory and empirical studies based on those theories is likely to have only limited applicability in linking information to quality. Although the evidence from such studies may at times be used to formulate guidelines for translating educational information into strategic decisions, one should not be limited to this approach because there are other ways to make those connections.

(b) Self-evident connections

A much more direct connection between educational information and educational decisions for raising quality can be established through "self-evident" links. These refer to links between various educational inputs and processes that are "logically" related to educational quality. The availability of information can strengthen policy development by exploiting these connections. Some simple examples of self-evident links have been presented below. Further examples can be found in Lockheed and Verspoor, (1989).

It is reasonable to believe that at least minimum levels of instructional materials such as paper, writing instruments, blackboards, chalk, and textbooks are necessary to support the learning process. In many developing countries, such materials are in short supply, particularly in rural areas. Indeed, there are classrooms where none of these are present. In such a situation the instructional process is handicapped considerably on *prima facie* grounds. Accordingly, it is important to collect information on the presence of such materials at the school site. Where materials availability is inadequate, it should be possible to raise quality through increasing these inputs. Even without a complete understanding of the effects of such classroom materials on learning, it is reasonable to use information on their availability to make decisions that can be linked to quality.

A similar case could be made for collecting and using information on such matters as student health status, student absenteeism, teacher absenteeism, and on teacher subject matter knowledge and training in the areas in which they are teaching. Even without evidence from educational production function studies or evaluations, it is reasonable to believe that each of these matters is linked to the quality of education because they represent fundamental preconditions for student learning. Accordingly, information on these matters can be helpful for decision-makers in assessing the present status of schools and in setting out strategies to raise quality.

(c) Practitioner knowledge

A third way of connecting information to strategies for improving the quality of education is through informing practitioners in ways that will assist and motivate them to change their own practices. A good example is the provision of detailed information from examinations that permits the matching of student performance on sub-tests and test items with corresponding aspects of curriculum, textbooks, instructional strategies, and teacher compentencies.

Typically, principals and teachers are given only broad examination results for their schools and students -- usually in the form of total test scores. If they were provided with more detailed information, they would be able to relate specific types of student performance to particular actions on their part. In this respect, an educational information system could link such information to quality by providing the practitioners with information that will enable them to change their own practices. Some of the knowledge that they might use to make these connections will be in the form of descriptive accounts setting out some "self-evident" examples of inputs and processes that might reasonably explain outcomes.

Practitioner knowledge, commonly described in general terms as "experience", also provides a basis for individual teachers to consider what works for them in a particular situation. That is, beyond the "self-evident" situation, they may have specific knowledge that helps them to use detailed information about their students in order to adapt the instructional process. For example, they may decide to spend more time on particular topics, to prepare special manipulable materials and examples to support learning, and to seek stronger ties between parents and the school -- all with a view to increasing learning in particular areas. These responses will generally be derived from previous experience in similar situations or from emulation of other successful practitioners in such situations. In some situations the changes that they make may be viewed as the basis for small "experiments" in which practitioners try different responses to see if they are effective, altering these responses over time if they are unsuccessful.

Conclusion

This chapter commenced with an exploration of the historical context of information's role in the management of education systems. It was argued that, in the 1980's, the "applied science" model of educational management had emerged as one of the dominant approaches adopted by practitioners. This model has extended the ways in which educational management has established linkages between information and the quality of education to methods that are quite often derived from the decision-maker's reflective considerations of personal participation in the field, and of continuing interaction with skilled practitioners.

The extension of methods for establishing linkages between information and the quality of education in this way has also extended the demand for the development of more extensive, and more imaginative, educational information systems than educational planners have used in the past. This demand has required educational planners to rethink exactly what information should be collected and then arranged it in formats that can be used by decision-makers. However, precise decisions about the content of educational information systems need to be made only after a comprehensive analysis of the information requirements of decision-makers. These matters have been taken up in detail in the following chapter.

Chapter 5

Issues in the design and development of educational information systems[1]

Introduction

Whatever linkages a decision-maker exploits between information and the quality of education, there are a number of matters that need to be addressed before educational planners commence to plan the collection and systematization of information. Initially, one needs to know who are the decision-makers, what "interests" in the education system do they have, and how these interests can be satisfied by information. When these questions have been answered, some questions that are more specific to the format, amount, and "side effects" of collecting the required information can then be considered.

Major issues

The decision-makers and their interests

In general terms there are four groups of people operating at different decision-making levels within most education systems: parents and teachers, school principals, state or provincial officials,

---

1. This chapter was prepared by Douglas Windham, Henry Levin and Zoltan Bathory.

and national officials. Each of these broad groups of people has a stake in the education system and is affected by the decisions that are made. Each of these groups also has a peculiar set of interests that may or may not be served by the educational system. For example, parents will be concerned about the educational performance of their own children. Teachers and other school staff will be concerned about curriculum, working conditions, community support, and career opportunities. School principals will have similar concerns as well as the level of resources and school performance. Provincial, state, and national officials will be concerned about efficiency in educational resource use and fairness in the distribution of the available resources. Finally, outside a direct role in decision-making, all members of society will have an interest in the degree to which the educational system delivers educational opportunities to all students and also provides programmes that will produce citizens who share a common culture and can be productive in the household, workplace, and their civic roles.

In some cases there may be considerable overlap in these interests, but in other cases interests may be in conflict. Even within each of the groups described above, there may be sub-groups with different educational interests. In addition, society in general may be fragmented into a variety of national, regional, and local sub-groups, each with different interests.

From interests to information

The important reason for identifying the broad groups of people described above is that differences in interests will generate very different questions about the status and performance of the educational system with accompanying differences in the types of information that will be needed to address these questions. The decisions taken at each decision-making level require specific information and the main purpose of an educational information system is, therefore, to provide relevant information to each group in an accurate and timely fashion, and in a form that is usable at the lowest possible cost.

An obvious implication arising from this situation is that different interests lead to different questions that are raised by the different groups. That is, for each constituency we can identify a set of interests that they have with respect to education and an associated set of questions. In an ideal situation each group would be privy to the particular types of information that are needed to make decisions concerning these questions in the most efficient and effective manner. However, things are hardly that simple. For example, consider the implication of designing and implementing an educational information system that provides useful data (a) for teachers and parents on the attractiveness of the educational process or experience, the educational options that students have and the quality of each, and future opportunities for graduating students, (b) for school principals on working conditions, curriculum, and educational goals, (c) for provincial and state officials on educational resources, and performance of the schools within their province and/or state, and (d) for national officials on the costs of education services, enrollments, student examination performance, teacher qualifications, and numbers of school staff.

In this illustration it is obvious that various complications will arise. Most importantly, the needs of the groups do not overlap. In the case of the teachers and parents, much of the information will be qualitative rather than quantitative, yet information systems are almost always quantitative with simple numerical measures of status rather than the provision of detailed descriptive information. The reasons for this are twofold.

First, not all constituencies are treated equally. In general, it is often assumed by Ministries of Education that the need for teachers and parents to have information is not of a high priority. Further, the collection of qualitative data on school experiences is costly and difficult to undertake. In contrast, it is usually assumed by Ministries of Education that the needs of educational administrators are of the highest importance. Moreover, the data required by administrators can usually be expressed in a numerical form -- suggesting a high level of precision and a relatively low cost to obtain and disseminate.

Second, what is collected primarily for one constituency is not necessarily of value for others. Thus, the notion of one comprehensive information system that will serve *all* needs is likely to be elusive. While some information might be needed in common by all groups, much of it will not be. Ultimately, choices have to be made on the matter of which group the information system will serve. It is better to be explicit about this at the design stage of an educational information system, rather than to suggest that one system can serve all interests.

One possible approach would be to rely mostly upon well-designed sample survey data for decisions at the national and state level, and leave the "full census" approach to the lower decision-making levels for which information is required about individual schools and students. A good probability sample with uniform measurement and data collection will, in many cases, provide superior national and state level information than by simply aggregating reports prepared by individual schools.

The format of information

An important part of translating interests into information is that the format of the information must suit the requirements of the decision-maker. In general, the concept of an "information system" almost invariably refers to numerical information that is made available in the form of printed and/or electronic archives, and also as reports for administrators at the top of an education system. Such information is usually not widely available in a form that would be considered meaningful to a wide range of constituencies. Nor does it normally include the types of information that can only be captured through descriptive printed materials, audiotapes, and videotapes. This limitation in the packaging and presentation of information results in the needs of many constituencies being ignored.

In order to circumvent the difficulties associated with the use of inappropriate formats for educational information, the following matters should be attended to in the design of information systems. First, the pertinent decision-makers should be identified in association with their interests in the educational system. Second, the appropriate types of information should be identified so that decision-makers can make informed decisions. Third, the format of the information that will be meaningful and accessible to decision-making groups should be identified. Fourth, an appropriate system of measurement, data collection, compilation, and distribution should be developed. Finally, the system should be implemented in a manner that will deliver information in a timely and accurate manner.

The purpose of setting out the features of an ideal educational information systems above was to illustrate the reality of how even the best educational system deviates substantially from the ideal ones. The best existing educational information systems provide a wide range of quantitative information in the form of electronic and print forms. The data are comprehensive with respect to the characteristics of the educational system including enrollments, staffing, costs, and educational outcomes. The data that they provide are reasonably timely and accurate in the sense that they are consistent with what they claim to measure. But such systems address primarily the needs of provincial, state, and national administrators rather than those of school principals, teachers, parents, or the community. By coincidence, some of the data may be of use to these other constituencies, but this usually represents a fortunate, but accidental, by-product rather than an intention.

At the very least, if an educational information system is to be used only for educational planning at provincial, state, and national levels, no pretense should be made that it is also being designed to serve parents, teachers, school principals, and so on, except to the degree that they are organized at regional and national levels. That is, individual parents, teachers, school principals, and members of the community are unlikely to be served by such an information system except through their collective representation by unions and regional or national organizations. However, it is important to note that even these organizations may be insensitive to the vast differences in data needs among their sub-populations.

The amount of information

In designing educational information systems, one must ask how much information to collect and disseminate. Clearly, the minimum amount of information that should be collected must be that which will respond to the needs of the various decision-making levels. There is a tendency among those who set out information requirements to specify their needs in great detail, less concerned with minimal data needs than with maximal ones. This tendency usually arises because bureaucrats are often seduced by the pressure to collect information that *might be used*, rather than information that *will be used*.

There are a number of reasons why this strategy is generally not appropriate. The first derives from the costs of information. The high fixed cost of establishing an information system means that the marginal cost of an additional piece of data is relatively small. Indeed, the average cost for each item of information will be a declining one up to a certain point. But, we must keep in mind that the first types of data that are specified are typically the easiest to measure and collect. As one addresses more detailed and finer-grained aspects, they become more difficult to specify and measure. Thus, there is a natural tendency for additional data to be associated with a rising marginal cost. Further, the more data that are collected, the more complex the information scheme, creating greater possibilities of confusion and error in both the assembly of the data and their use. From the cost-perspective, the amount of information that is collected should be large enough to spread the fixed costs of the information system over enough items to reduce the cost per item to a minimum; but it should not be so great that the marginal costs of additional items rise exorbitantly and the information system becomes unwieldy and error-prone.

If possible, the additional value of any particular item of information that is to be collected should justify its cost. Michael Scriven has embodied this notion into educational evaluation by calling it cost-free evaluation (Scriven, 1980; 1983). That is, the investment required to obtain educational information that can be used for decisions must be, at least, offset by the benefits of making better decisions. While this principle is a difficult one to operationalize -- since the information system must be designed and implemented before any benefits can be derived and measured -- it is an important one to keep in mind. A particularly crucial point in this context is to remember that additional items of information are often characterized by diminishing marginal usefulness. For example, Cronbach and Gleser (1965) have demonstrated that at some point additional items of test information will be characterized by diminishing marginal utility. Although test makers like to add such items because they believe that the reliability of the test increases according to its length, such increases become smaller and smaller with each added item until they become negligible.

The "Side effects" of information collection

One major impact of an educational information system is that it may define the focus of decision-makers in ways that were not anticipated. For example, if an information system emphasizes student participation rates and enrolments, local reporting systems may tend to overstate such phenomena by counting non-participants as participants and so on. This is particularly true if fiscal and other incentives are related to the reports.

One example that is prominent in industrialized countries is the tendency to "teach towards the test" in order to maximize examination scores. Even when the precise examination questions are not known by the teachers, the format is generally standardized. Thus, it is not uncommon for schools to give their students considerable practice in answering questions that are framed in the format of the test rather than in more natural contexts. Students may be given vocabulary words and their definitions to memorize, ignoring the fact that the meaning of language comes from its context. Thus, the learning will be artifical and designed to do well on examinations rather than in showing students how to deduce meaning from context.

In more extreme cases, schools will require students to memorize exercises that have appeared on previous versions of examinations. In the process, the schools develop a mechanical set of techniques for maximizing examination scores rather than focussing their programmes and teaching techniques on the kinds of more meaningul learning experiences that examinations are supposed to reflect. These kinds of distortions can be turned to creative ends that will improve the quality of education by re-casting examinations into formats that reflect meaningful learning of higher order skills rather than trivial memorization. This approach will be enhanced if examination questions are changed considerably from year to year so that teachers are forced to teach the higher order skills that are required to *understand* the questions -- rather than using the items themselves to design the curriculum.

The development of educational information systems

Essential first steps

(a) Information needs

The critical task in designing effective educational information systems is the definition of information needs. This can be done in one of three ways. First, information can be collected because "it has always been collected" and/or because it is relatively easy to collect (the traditional emphasis on enrollment data versus achievement data is explainable in this way). Second, one can conduct a "felt-need" analysis of major decision-makers in which one asks them to articulate the types of information concerning the quality of education that they require and to assign priorities among the information types. Third, one can impose on the system a set of criteria based on theory and experience, but related more to what the management theorist feels is needed, rather than what current or potential users request. This last alternative is often very important because many decision-makers at all levels of education systems do not have sufficient experience with measures of the quality of education to articulate their needs in advance. Auditing data use over time will allow for further future refinements in the definition of the information system to fit users needs. The final result should combine the advantages of continuity and low cost with user and conceptually defined needs in a manner that maximizes the utility of information provision for quality enhancement.

(b) Training needs

One must accept the fact that within complex organizations like education systems one will find educational planners and decision-makers who lack the training necessary to do their job. Educational bureaucracies in both the developed and developing world are characterized by large numbers of middle-level managers who have had neither formal nor on-the-job training concomitant with their responsibilities. In such a situation it is necessary to develop a means for identifying the data needs of an information system that is not solely dependent on expressed user needs.

The training of data and information suppliers and users has been a challenge faced by all those who desire to improve organizational or system effectiveness, but it has posed special problems in the education and human resource sectors because of the large numbers of managerial or administrative personnel, the complexity of the choices they face, and the frequent inappropriateness or irrelevance of their previous training. The latter issue is a problem whether administrators are former teachers without training, or professional managers without classroom or school administrative experience.

In general terms, there are four main categories of training that educational planners require in order to be able to articulate their information needs and to be able to use their information for decision-making purposes: (i) specific management skill training, (ii) training in the conceptual framework of education cost and effectiveness analysis, (iii) training in logic and data-based argument, and iv) training in the application of these skills, concepts, and logic to the requirements of their jobs.

(c) Specification of benchmarks

In association with appropriate training for educational planners and decision-makers, education systems aiming to improve the quality of education need to establish agreed benchmarks for "quality" and then set up appropriate monitoring systems to assess the performance of the various educational programmes and projects conducted by the system against these benchmarks.

Because of bureaucratic reluctance to expose programmes and activities to review and evaluation, macro-educational quality reforms can generally only proceed through a commitment of the most senior officials of an education system to an emphasis on quality considerations. These very senior officials will often need to re-orient the attitudes of their staff from a view of the evaluation of quality as a forensic exercise designed to identify past culpability and assign blame, towards an acceptance of it as a standard procedure for identifying the means for improving operations and for assigning rewards for actions resulting in improvements. To achieve this change in attitude will require that the reformers overcome aspects of both bureaucratic tradition and normal human psychology so that the mode of operation for the education system is collective responsibility for future improvement rather than individual blame for past shortcomings.

Developmental levels for educational information systems

A macro-educational information system that would be suitable for planning the quality of education should be organized around the following seven categories of data:

- Student characteristics
- Teacher and administrator characteristics
- Curriculum, educational materials and instructional practice
- Facilities and equipment
- Attainment and achievement data
- Education and training outcomes
- Costs

An inherent part of the macro-educational policy process should be a periodic review and modification of data collected under these categories. As a data system and its users become more mature with respect to their capacity to formulate meaningful questions focussed on the quality of education, more complex statistics can be introduced. The actual progress of a system will depend on where it begins (in terms of data quality and decision-maker capacities), the resources made available, and the importance assigned by decision-makers to quality considerations. While substantial variation will occur from nation to nation, *Tables 3.1 to 3.3* (from Windham, 1988) present three levels of development that an educational information system might follow.

The stages described by these tables are not fixed in their details nor would they necessarily be distinct in their implementation. The initial degree of detail will be a function of the state of development of any existing system. In the progression from the first to the third levels the data will increase in coverage, accuracy and interpretability. The interpretability gains will occur in part because of a greater capacity to assimilate data through comparison and contrast of data sets. For example, gender ratios and student outcome measures, etc. can be combined with teacher characteristics by region and across time to provide information that would be suitable for guiding a discussion of whether having more women teachers tends to be associated with (in either a coincidental or causal linkage) the tendency for greater attendance, retention, and measured achievement by female students.

Table 3.1: First level development of benchmarks for an educational
information system

Major Area	Sub-Area
Student Data	- Enrollment by school - Gender ratios - Progression rates (aggregate only)
Administrator and Teacher Data	- Distribution by qualifications - Distribution by location - Student-Teacher ratios
Curriculum/Educational Materials	- Textbook availability - Regional and size-of-place distribution
Facilities/Equipment	- Number of "complete" schools - Students per school - Students per class
Attainment/Achievement	- National examination pass rates - Promotion rates
Outcomes	- No data
Costs	- Teacher salaries by qualifications - Aggregate budget data - Cost per student by level of education

Table 3.2: Second level development of benchmarks for an educational
information system

Major Area	Sub-Area
(All level one data plus the following)	
Student Data	- Gender data cross-tabulated with size-of-place and region
	- Ethnic distributions
	- Detail by level and type of programme
	- Separate repetition and attrition rates
	- Age distributions
Administrator and Teacher Data	- Qualifications distribution including specialisations
Curriculum/Educational Materials	- Knowledge of curriculum by administrators and teachers
	- Users' evaluations of curriculum and materials
	- Evaluation of alternative instructional technologies
Facilities/Equipment	- Equipment utilization
	- Needs analysis
	- Maintenance and replacement projections
Attainment/Achievement	- Determinants of educational outputs
	- Determinants of inequalities
	- Analysis of high and low achieving schools
Outcomes	- Net present value estimates of lifetime income gains by level and type of education
	- Studies of graduate attitudes and behaviors
	- Job search rates by level and type of graduate
Costs	- Detailed cost analyses of major programmes and alternative technologies
	- Cost projections by level and type of education

Table 3.3: Third level development of benchmarks for an educational
             information system

Major Area	Sub-Area
(All level one and two data plus the following)	
Student data	- Subject or course specializations
	- Attitudinal and behavioral measures
	- Time utilization
Administrator and Teacher Data	- Time utilization
	- Training needs
	- Interaction with community
	- Job satisfaction
Curriculum/Educational Materials	- Knowledge of curriculum by administrators and teachers
	- Users' evaluations of curriculum and materials
	- Evaluation of alternative instructional technologies
Facilities/Equipment	- Equipment utilization
	- Needs analysis
	- Maintenance and replacement projections
Attainment/Achievement	- Determinants of educational outputs
	- Determinants of inequalities
	- Analysis of high and low achieving schools
Outcomes	- Net present value estimates of lifetime income gains by level and type of education
	- Studies of graduate attitudes and behaviors
	- Job search rates by level and type of graduate
Costs	- Detailed cost analyses of major programmes and alternative technologies
	- Cost projections by level and type of education

The rate of increase in detail and coverage between the three
levels of development will vary among the individual categories of
data. In most countries student, teacher, and administrator data will
be emphasised while in others the focus may be on costs or on
facilities and equipment utilization. While variation in rates of
change in the data groups is unavoidable, it still may be a matter of
management concern. For example, if cost detail exceeds information
on input quality or on output and outcome effectiveness, this
condition can give rise to serious efficiency misinterpretations. The
goal of the benchmark structure should be to emphasize a balanced
development across the seven data categories so that comparability in
detail, coverage, and accuracy promote improved interpretability for
policy purposes of the total operation.

Data detail also may be expected to vary by level and type of education or training. Because of the increased level of operating expenses, one may expect a greater availability of cost detail to emerge in the higher education and vocational training subsectors. Because of the political and social importance of concerns with basic educational opportunity, the measures of gender, ethnicity, isolation, and regional equity in access and retention may be collected in greater detail at the pre-primary and primary educational levels. However, even these patterns of data detail by level and type of education will vary from country to country and over time.

Unfortunately, educational information system specialists have had little experience in meeting the needs of decision-makers at microeducational levels. A major area of needed research (to parallel the current macro-educational work of Unesco, OECD and specific developed nations such as France and the United States) is to identify the nature of data needed by students, families, communities, teachers, and school administrators in their decision-making about educational quality. A major aspect of this research will be the need to develop congruence between the data base for macro- and micro-educational decision-making. This will be possible only to the extent that human and financial capacity allow use of new data assimilation technologies and that macro-educational decision-making becomes more concerned with the variety of educational realities rather than average or modal forms of educational phenomena.

In summary, the data forms in a quality-based educational information system must be concerned with utilization of resources and their interaction, effectiveness in achieving learning outputs (including noncognitive goals), and efficiency. In this last case, a special emphasis must be placed on *detailed cost data* as opposed to *aggregate expenditure data*. The costs of education, in both public and private institutions, often far exceed the "formal" public expenditure allocated to education. Costs (the valuation of all resources contributed to an activity regardless of their source) are the most underdeveloped part of most educational information systems. Unit costs (normally defined as per-student) and cycle costs (per graduate or successful completor) are a necessary part of any evaluation of the relative efficiency of an educational activity. Also, incorporation of private and community contributions to education is essential since these funds frequently are a critical determinant of quality and, perhaps more importantly, of variations in quality within and among schools and schools systems.

To be of decision-making value, educational cost information must be disaggregated at the macro-level by educational cycle, programme type, and for specific client populations, and at micro-levels for the specific educational alternatives available to individuals and communities. The work of Tsang (1988) illustrates the gap between the current level of data sophistication in most countries and the potential value of more appropriate cost estimates in educational decision-making. Cost, like equity, must be an explicit consideration of any discussion concerning the quality of education (Windham, 1990).

The costs of educational information systems

An important set of investment issues revolves around the technical and resource constraints associated with constructing educational information systems in developing countries. Technical constraints refer to shortages of trained personnel and infrastructure for establishing and maintaining educational information in a usable form. This does not mean that the establishment of such a system is an impossible task for a developing country, but it does mean it will be difficult and will probably require assistance from outside experts during the initial stages.

Resource constraints in most developing countries during the early 1990's will be so severe as to limit expenditure to a continuation of what is already in place. For many of these countries any new initiative, such as the construction of a highly articulated and detailed information system, will need to be supported by arguments that the benefits and returns that can be attributed to information are so high as to justify the costs. Obviously, these arguments must be settled by evidence from concrete situations, but it should be noted that provision of additional resources to construct and maintain a more extensive information system should be justified on *both* economic and educational grounds.

It is entirely possible that the same resources would provide a greater contribution to educational quality when spent on educational materials, teachers' salaries, and better school management. Clearly, some minimal amount of information on enrolments, expenditures, staffing, facilities, and outcomes is necessary to undertake a basic monitoring of the educational system. The issue is *how much* one is willing to invest to make the information more accurate and extensive. This is a marginal investment decision in which the value of the additional investment in gathering more accurate and extensive information must be weighed against other uses for the same resources.

In summary, educational information must be subject to the same cost effectiveness criterion that should be applied to all considerations of educational inputs and processes. However, one must avoid sacrificing long-term information system needs on the basis of short-term information utilization criteria. The need for time series to monitor quality benchmarks and for comparability among areas and over time may require a short-term excess capacity in order to meet long-term requirements. Where long-term efficiency places a burden on short-term affordability for the least advantaged areas and nations, special assistance will again be required from international assistance agencies and by central government agencies.

Operationalizing a cost-effective educational information system will be facilitated to the extent that at least some form of core data set for use by decision-makers at different levels of the educational system can be identified and created. Further, cost containment alternatives for information investments in education can be achieved by the wider user of sampling rather than census methods, the creation and discontinuation of special data series in line with special needs, and the incorporation of separately-funded research findings in the information system both as a supplement to current data and as a means of identifying new data needs. Similarly, improved horizontal integration (across agencies and ministries) can help reduce new cost demands while maintaining the vertical integration of information among decision-makers at all levels.

Conclusion

A number of the conceptual foundations of this chapter will be elaborated in the discussions that follow on the specific technical and contextual requirements for the construction of information systems aimed at improving the quality of education. However, this initial discussion has pointed the way to some specific needs that must be dealt with.

First, the implementation of a programme focussed on planning the quality of education will require extensive training of both those who supply and those who use the new information on education. Second, assistance will be needed in the design of information systems to serve decision-makers operating at different levels of an education system and to provide new forms of information on costs, resource utilization, classroom and school processes, and a variety of school outcomes. And, third, a restructuring of educational authority and responsibility will be needed to empower decision-making by those individuals and authorities who are best informed about specific educational quality needs and the alternatives for educational policies and practices.

As a final comment it should be stated that however well an educational information system is designed and operationalized its effects on educational quality will be determined by the organizational and policy context within which it is operationalized. A cost-effective approach focussed on quality is almost certainly a prerequisite for planning quality enhancement above a rudimentary level; but it is not by any means sufficient in and of itself to assure that improved planning of education or enhanced quality of educational operations will result. Quality improvements ultimitantly must depend on the broadest considerations of the surrounding culture, politics, and economics. Educational information systems developed without such consideration cannot serve the needs of decision-makers except those who define their interests in the narrowest, bureaucratic context.

Part III
Improving the collection and use
of educational information

Chapter 6

Improving data collection, preparation, and analysis procedures: a review of technical issues[1]

Introduction

Improving the collection, preparation, and analysis of data that are required to guide decisions aimed at improving the quality of education requires, in addition to a concern about the scope of the data collection, careful design and management of the data collection and preparation procedures (especially in the areas of sampling, instrumentation, field work, data entry and data preparation), and appropriate data analysis and reporting.

These concerns are related through the costs involved in each, with a tradeoff between scope (broad targets for, and the frequency of, data collection) and depth (the complexity of the data collection instruments and related data collection process). That is, a decision to collect data must be informed by prior decisions regarding the units of observation (how many), the questions to be answered (how many), and the resources available for data collection. In general, for the same costs, more questions may be asked of fewer respondents or fewer questions may be asked of more respondents. Common errors in data collection often arise from a desire to collect more

---

1. This chapter was prepared by Kenneth Ross, T. Neville Postlethwaite, Marlaine Lockheed, Aletta Grisay and Gabriel Carceles Breis.

information from more respondents than resources realistically permit

This chapter is focused mainly on the technical issues that often arise after the initial decisions have been taken with respect to what data should be collected. However, it is important to note that decisions taken concerning what data should be collected need to be supported by an explanation of why these data are be collected and how these data are to be collected, prepared, analysed, and then used by decision-makers operating at various planning levels of an education system.

In essence, improving the collection, preparation and analysis of data requires attention to detail. That is, there are no "shortcuts" to achieving high standards in these areas. However, there are many easy ways to ensure that standards are low and that the results of the data analyses are meaningless. In the following sections of this chapter a discussion of some of the technical issues associated with data collection, preparation and analysis have been presented within a framework that puts the "*basic requirements*" for success alongside the authors' observations, in both developed and developing countries, of "*what often happens*" to prevent success. The chapter concludes with an exploration of "*what might be done in future*" -- especially in terms of training programmes designed to improve the capacity of educational planners to undertake productive projects in this area. While the paper concentrates on the features of survey sample approaches, many of the issues raised are pertinent to most data collection activities -- including censuses.

The scope of the data collection

The first issue to be decided before any data are collected, is the scope of the data collection. That is, an initial decision must be taken with respect to the question: "Information about what?". For example, are data to be collected for a whole population (of say schools, teachers, or students) or is a probability sample to be selected from a well-defined target population? Data collection efforts in many countries concentrate on enumerating the population of students, teachers and schools. This is a decision that, because of the breadth/depth tradeoff, yields little information about many units. Some data on the entire population (that is, a census) need to be collected regularly in order to inform managerial decisions, such as the allocation of resources. These types of data include the total number of students, teachers, and schools. In some countries, data on student populations are required in order to monitor compliance with compulsory education laws.

For most purposes, sample surveys with units sampled from sampling frames developed for a well-defined target population are sufficient. Sample surveys, when designed and executed appropriately, can provide as much information as complete censuses, at considerably less cost. For example, sample surveys are often adequate for providing accurate estimates of enrolment rates, and are virtually mandatory for estimating national achievement levels, particularly for students in grades not regularly examined for selection purposes.

Whether a decision is made to use a census or a sample, it is important to ensure that data that are collected can be reported as quickly as possible. The collection of too many data for too many units may be counter-productive because it may result in delays in the final reporting of results. This is clearly unsatisfactory because decision-makers need to obtain a clear picture of the current state of an education system before considering the particular policy measures required to improve the quality of education. In situations where time-series data is being used, this is extremely important because decision-makers will be analyzing trends in the data and they need to know quickly if some overall trend downwards, or upwards, in the quality of education has occurred.

The sample design

Due to practical constraints on research resources, data collections that include an assessment of educational outcomes for students are usually restricted to the study of a sample rather than a complete coverage of the population for which these generalizations are required. Provided that scientific sampling procedures are used, the use of a sample often provides a number of advantages compared with a census. For example, reduced costs associated with all aspects of data collection and analysis, reduced requirements for specialized personnel to conduct the field work, greater speed in most aspects of data manipulation and summarization, and greater accuracy due to the possibility of closer supervision of the fieldwork. Samples are perfectly adequate for describing most characteristics of an education system. In fact most analytic work depends upon samples, even when census type data are available because the computational requirements for analyzing complete population data are often very large.

Good sample designs for studies of educational outcomes do not occur by chance -- they are constructed by using established sampling procedures in association with a practical knowledge of the ways in which populations of schools, teachers, and students are administratively and geographically arranged. While the optimal sample design for a particular data collection in a particular country will always contain many unique features, the basic requirements listed in the following section are common to most well-designed samples.

Sample design: basic requirements

(a) *Target population definitions.* Descriptions should be prepared for the desired target population (the population for which results are ideally required), the defined target population (the population which is actually studied and whose elements have a known and non-zero chance of being selected into the sample), and the excluded population (the population comprised of the elements excluded from the desired target population in order to form the defined target population).

(b) *Specification of domains and strata.* The domains for the data collection (the sub-populations for which separate estimates are specifically planned) should be nominated. The stratification variables should then be selected and justified in terms of gains in sampling precision.

(c) *Sampling error requirements.* The required level of sampling precision (the permissible boundaries of sampling error associated with sample estimates of important population parameters) should be established and this should be checked against prevailing administrative, financial, and political constraints.

(d) *Size of sample.* The size of the sample should be calculated by using information concerning the proposed sample design (the number of stages of selection in the sample design, the stratification procedures, the nature of the primary sampling units, the magnitude of the coefficient of intraclass correlation and/or the design effect), the required level of sampling precision (see above), and the proposed data collection environment (for example, the numbers of students per school that, under standardized conditions, can be administered the instruments associated with the data collection).

(e) *Sampling frame*. The sampling frame should be constructed for the defined target population in separate parts representing the strata. Appropriate measure of size figures (Kish, 1965: 222) should be assigned, and then a check should be made to ensure that the total and stratum subtotal numbers of students in the frame are in accord with the numerical description of the defined target population.

(f) *Mechanical selection procedure*. A suitable mechanical selection procedure (Kish, 1965: 26) should be applied in order to select the sample members from the sampling frame with known probabilities of selection.

(g) *Sampling weights and sampling errors*. Appropriate sampling weight calculations and sampling error estimation techniques should be selected in order to cope with any complexities (stratification, multiple stages, clustering) that have been introduced into the sample design.

Sample design: what often happens

(a) *The defined target population and the excluded population are never clearly defined.* This may arise because the researcher either does not bother to specify the size and nature of these populations or, due mainly to confusion, is unable to provide precise definitions. Unfortunately, this problem often goes hand-in-hand with the researcher making generalizations about a desired target population that, upon careful scrutiny, consists mostly of the excluded population.

(b) *The participants in the study are nominated rather than sampled.* This approach is often justified in terms of cost or accessibility considerations, however both of these "constraints" can usually be addressed by adjusting the defined target population definition and then applying appropriate stratification procedures. These non-probability samples, sometimes referred to as "nominated samples", are generally described in scientifically meaningless terms such as "quota", "representative", "purposive", "expert choice", or "judgemental" samples. Kish (1965) characterized data collections based on this approach as "investigations" and pointed out that they should not be confused with appropriately designed experiments or surveys. The main problems associated with the use of nominated samples are that it is not possible to estimate the sampling errors or to have any idea of the magnitude of the bias associated with the selection procedures (Brickell,1974). Consequently, nominated samples should be used only for the trial-testing of instrumentation or new curriculum materials because in these activities it is sometimes desirable to employ a "distorted" sample that has, for example, a disproportionately large number of students at the extremes of a spectrum of ability, ethnicity, socio-economic status, etc.

(c) *The sampling frame is faulty because it is out of date and/or is incomplete and/or has duplicate entries.* The construction and maintenance of a comprehensive sampling frame for schools, teachers, and students may be neglected because it is considered to be too expensive or because the systematic collection of official statistics in a country is error-prone. This is sometimes the situation in countries where population growth rates are high and where large and uncontrolled movements of population from rural to urban settings are commonplace. However, there are also a number of countries that are unable to provide accurate information in this area because the management and financing of schooling is undertaken by local communities, or because there is an independently managed non-government school sector. The researcher faced with these difficulties often proceeds to use a faulty sampling frame based on poor quality official statistics in the mistaken belief that there are no other alternatives. In fact there are well-established solutions to these problems that employ "area sampling" (Ross, 1986) and, provided that a trained team of "enumerators" is available to list schools within selected areas, it is possible to prepare a high quality sample design without having access to an accurate sampling frame based on a listing of individual schools.

(d) *Confusion surrounding the terms "total sample size" and "effective sample size" results in the total sample size for a complex cluster sample being set at the wrong level either by the use of simple random sampling assumptions or, quite frequently, by guesswork.* In school systems that are highly "streamed", either explicitly on the basis of test scores or implicitly through the residential segregation of socio-economic groups, the use of complex cluster sampling can have dramatic effects on the total sample size that is required to reach a specific level of sampling precision. Researchers with a limited knowledge of this situation often employ simple random sampling assumptions for the estimation of the required total sample size. In order to illustrate the dangers associated with a lack of experience in these matters, consider the following two examples based on schools in a country where the intraclass correlation for achievement scores at the Grade 6 level is around 0.6 for intact classes. A sample of 40 classes with 25 students selected per class would provide a total sample size of 1000 students -- however this sample would only provide similar sampling errors as a simple random sample of 65 students when estimating the average population achievement level! Further, a sample of 50 classes with 4 students selected per class would provide a total sample size of "only 200 students" but would nevertheless provide estimates that were more precise than the above sample of 1000 students!

(e) *The wrong formulae are used for the calculation of sampling errors and/or for the application of tests of significance.* This usually occurs when the researcher employs a complex cluster sample (for example, by selecting intact classes within schools) and then uses the sampling error formulae appropriate for simple random sampling to calculate the sampling errors (Ross, 1985). The most extreme form of this mistake occurs when differences in means and/or percentages are described as being "important" or "significant" without providing any sampling error estimates at all -- not even the incorrect ones! These kinds of mistakes are quite common -- especially where "treatment versus control" comparisons are being made in order to compare, for example, current practices with new curriculum content or new teaching materials (Ross, 1987).

(f) *The researcher has undertaken a few hours of training in sampling as part of a "research methods" course and this provides just enough knowledge and personal confidence to precipitate the occurrence of major errors.* The five errors that have been observed most often by the authors have been listed below.

- *Population size and sample size.* A researcher uses the once-fashionable sampling approach of basing sample size on a fixed percentage of the population size because he believes that a large population requires a large sample, and vice versa. In fact, for most surveys in educational research, the finite population correction factor in sampling error formulae is very close to one and therefore the population size need not be considered when planning the size of the sample.

- *Bias adjustment for non-response.* A researcher designs a sample so that it is 25 percent larger than required in order to cope with an expected response rate of around 70 to 80 percent. This approach may deliver a final sample with the required total sample size, but it will not guarantee freedom from bias because non-response is often associated with a sub-population that has unique characteristics. A failure to understand this point is due to confusion between two independent sources of "total error": sampling error and bias.

- *Units of sampling and units of analysis.* A researcher employs a commonly-used sample design based on a probability proportional to size sample of schools followed by a simple random sample of a fixed number of students in each sample school. This sample design is self-weighting for students and therefore the between-student data analyses are reasonably straightforward. However at the between-school level of analysis caution needs to shown with respect to interpreting univariates based on weighted and unweighted school means (Kish, 1965: 186).

- *Bias in selection.* A researcher has an accurate list of schools to use for a sampling frame and proceeds to select a simple random sample of schools followed by the selection of a simple random sample of a fixed number of students within each selected school. The researcher then proceeds to conduct unweighted data analyses without realizing that the sampling procedures have given students in smaller schools a much higher chance of selection than students in larger schools.

- *Sampling errors output by the standard statistical software packages.* A researcher conducts a survey using a sample of students selected as intact class groups and then uses a statistical software package (for example, SAS, SPSS, BMDP, or MINITAB) to conduct significance tests on the differences in two sample means. The test statistics that are provided in the computer output are likely to be incorrect because they will be based on formulae that assume simple random sampling.

The design of data collection instruments

Data collection requires the use of some medium for "collecting" data: notebooks, questionnaires, optical scanning forms, and in some cases microcomputers used in the field. The type of data collection instrument will determine the type of data preparation required before the data analyses. Open-ended questionnaires or interviews require more preparation effort than do pre-coded questionnaires, and pre-coded questionnaires require more than questionnaires that are designed for optical scanning, which, in turn, require more attention to data preparation than do data that are directly entered into a microcomputer.

Data collection instruments: basic requirements

The data collection instruments should be clear in terms of the information they seek, retain data disaggregated at an appropriate level, and permit the matching of data within hierarchically designed samples or across time. Furthermore, they must be designed to permit subsequent statistical analysis of data for reliability and (if possible) validity. In this chapter, it is not appropriate to describe in great detail the procedures for good instrument development. However, the basic requirements are that the questions posed do not present problems of interpretation to the respondent, and that, when forced choice options are provided, the choices are mutually exclusive and are likely to discriminate among respondents. Since in most countries, mainframe computers permit the storage of data at considerable levels of disaggregation, data collection instruments need to allow for this level of disaggregation. If hierarchically designed samples are developed (containing, for example, data for students, their teachers, their schools, their parents, etc.) and the merging of data from different sources is required for data analysis, then the instruments must include appropriate identifying numbers for linking the different sources of data.

Data collection instruments: what often happens

(a) *Poor physical layout.* Many data collection instruments reflect a desire to reduce costs at the outset through limiting the amount of paper used. The result is that questions are shortened to the degree that their meaning is unclear, response alternatives in forced choice questions are not elaborated to the degree that their meaning is clear, information is crammed into sheets of paper with little concern for subsequent data preparation and coding. The result of a poor layout is that considerable errors are introduced into the data. For example, a school survey in Africa listed all household members on a single sheet of paper, but data about each member were entered, in some cases, vertically on the paper and in other cases, horizontally. To enter the data into the computer from this form would have taken more time than to have recopied the data into another instrument.

(b) *Lack of question pretesting.* Pretesting questions is a necessary step in instrument development, and one that is frequently overlooked. The result of a failure to pretest is that respondents (particularly in a large sample survey, where an individual "enumerator" is not available to clarify matters) can be confused by a question, and answer inappropriately. When obtaining measures of student achievement, pretesting is absolutely necessary so that items may be checked for their difficulty and discrimination levels. If items are either too hard or too easy, there will be little discrimination in the resulting test score. Where open-ended responses are to be subsequently coded into categories, pretesting can assist in the development of the categories, or can even lead to eliminating the need for a separate coding step. For example, in one international survey, students were asked to indicate the total number of brothers and sisters in their family. The question was asked in the form of a forced choice response with the maximum value being "five or more" and in several countries more than 80 percent of the children indicated this category as their choice. Pretesting would have indicated the need to extend the number of categories to allow for the very large family sizes in these countries, or to leave the question open-ended.

(c) *Failure to use technology*. The use of some types of technology can reduce errors associated with data preparation. For example, optical scanning sheets when used in appropriate situations can be read by an optical scanner much more quickly than printed instruments can be hand coded, the use of this type of technology can reduce the length of time between data collection and analysis. Other types of technology, such as using microcomputers in the field for entering data, can also improve the quality of data collections.

The management of the data collection

The management of the data collection requires the researcher to arrange for a standardized administration of the research instruments (tests, questionnaires, etc.) to the persons selected into the sample. In practice, this means that the researcher, or a suitably trained field-worker, will go to the school and administer the relevant instruments in the manner prescribed by the research design to the appropriate students, and, in some cases, to the appropriate teachers, school principals, parents, and community leaders. There may also be a requirement for the recording of observational data concerning classroom teaching, school management, environmental conditions, etc. In large studies of educational outcomes, for example the "Indonesian Quality of Education Study" (Postlethwaite and Ross, 1987), all of the data sources listed above will be involved and will be intimately interconnected in the sense that it will be important to be able to link each student's data with the data describing his/her own classmates, teacher, school principal, parent, and community leader.

In the following discussion, some of the basic requirements associated with conducting an effective data collection for a study of educational outcomes have been outlined. These requirements are centred around the need for the principal researcher to maintain control of field operations through an effective management plan and the use of high quality field manuals.

Data collection: basic requirements

(a) *Maintenance of control over the execution of the sample design in the field*. All persons involved in the field work should understand that the researcher is the only person who has the authority to nominate the various sampling units for inclusion or exclusion. This requires that the researcher should supervise the preparation of an unambiguous list of the *names* of the schools to be involved in the data collection and then, following a preliminary visit to the nominated schools by an trained enumerator, the researcher should supervise the preparation of an unambiguous list of the *names* of the students to be involved. Detailed instructions should also be prepared so that there is no doubt as to identity of any other persons (teachers, school principals, etc.) that are to be included in the data collection.

(b) *The role of the researcher in the data collection.* Sustained staff enthusiasm is essential in order to ensure the success of the data collection and this can only be achieved if the researcher gets involved with the work at all levels. "Getting involved" means doing much more than giving speeches, writing papers, circulating memos, or talking on the telephone -- it means taking personal responsibility for day-to-day practical operations and actually doing some of the less glamorous research tasks. For example: participating in the training of the field workers, helping with some of the field work, making personal visits to sample schools that may be reluctant to take part in the data collection, being accessible to staff and showing appreciation for their good work, meeting regularly with supervisory staff in order to monitor progress.

(c) *The preparation of field manuals.* The data collection at the school level should be planned in great detail and these plans should be outlined in two easily-understood field manuals: the "School Co-ordinator's Manual" and the "Test Administrator's Manual". The School Co-ordinator's Manual should describe every step to be taken by the person responsible for the data collection in each school -- from the time the instruments arrive in the school to the time they are packaged and returned to the central research office. In some situations this will be the School Principal, or a teacher in the school appointed by the school principal. In other situations it will be a field worker appointed by the researcher to go to the school in order to arrange the data collection. In both situations the manual needs to be written so that the School Co-ordinator is absolutely clear about what is required to be achieved and this should be reinforced by providing a training programme during which all of the materials to used in the data collection are presented and explained clearly. The Test

Administrator's Manual should be a separate document from the School Co-ordinator's Manual in order to cover the situation where someone other than the School Co-ordinator is to be responsible for the administration of the data collection instruments. In order to standardize the administration conditions across all of the data collection points, the Test Administrators Manual should be written in the form of a scripted play (with prompts) so that there is little, or no, opportunity for the Test Administrator to confuse the respondents. If observation schedules are to be used in the data collection, these two manuals will need to be supplemented by further training which includes inter-rater reliability investigations.

Data collection: what often happens

(a) *The researcher is unable to manage the project after it has been launched and therefore cannot monitor daily data collection operations in a manner that will permit timely and effective responses to be made to major crises.* The main reasons for these difficulties are usually associated with the following four areas. Each area has been illustrated with examples that have been observed by the authors.

- *Inadequate training and/or experience.* The researcher has either never been trained in the techniques of data collection or has had some theoretical training but no practical experience. For example: A government engineer working on projects that were mainly concerned with road construction was suddenly told, because an international aid agency had requested an evaluation of several of its projects, to conduct a series of large-scale educational evaluation studies. A second example: an education ministry official returned to work, after completing a Ph.D. based on a study of the linguistic development of eight children, and was directed to undertake a national evaluation programme for all of the core subjects in each grade level of primary schools.

- *Professional status.* Professional status sometimes prevents the researcher from getting involved with the mundane but difficult aspects of the data collection and consequently when "real" problems arise in the field he/she is not able to respond with a workable solution because of an incapacity to understand the difficulties in practical terms. For example: A researcher was required to supervise the data preparation for a national testing programme involving ten thousand students but would not acknowledge that he needed to do some of the data preparation himself in order to know how to train and supervise the team selected to do the work. A second example: A researcher chose to participate in the field work for a few first-class schools in the wealthy neighbourhoods of a province that was known internationally for its excellent tourist attractions, fine cuisine, and first class hotels. The data collection for these schools was found to be running smoothly, and the researcher returned home after having a relaxing and comfortable "holiday" -- but without getting any first-hand knowledge of the kinds of difficulties that were being experienced by his own field workers in other provinces.

- *Too many jobs.* The capacity of well-qualified and experienced people in developing countries to do research is often diminished for two main reasons. First, people with this high level of training are in short supply and therefore they are always being asked by their governments to take responsibility for a range of administrative tasks and a large number of research studies. Second, these people, mainly through education and travel, have often acquired a taste for a life-style that exceeds the buying power of their official government salaries with the result that they become involved in "outside work" for both the government and the private sector. For example: A researcher, having completed a Ph.D. that included training in most aspects of survey research methods, was given responsibility for supervising the data collection for one of the largest studies of elementary schooling ever conducted. At the same time he was the principal researcher for another large project, a part-time lecturer at two universities and a community college, a paid member of a range of advisory committees for other large research projects, an active partner in a private consultancy company working on various large-scale contract research tasks, a member of committees responsible for drafting government policy papers, a "counterpart" for a constant stream of overseas consultants, and was also required to prepare answers to Ministerial requests for information on education.

- *Communication difficulties.* In some countries the standard forms of communication (mail, telephone, telex, etc.) are often inaccessible or not operating effectively. Consequently, it is not always possible for problems in the field to be conveyed to the researcher in good time to attend to difficulties before they begin to disrupt the data collection. Some of these problems cannot be anticipated in advance and therefore they cannot be included in either the School Co-ordinator's Manual or the Test Administrator's Manual. For example: A field worker travelled to a sample school in a remote part of a country and found that the data collection could not proceed for two sample schools because one was closed when the teacher left without informing the Ministry of Education, and the other did not exist because the buildings had recently been destroyed by a landslide. Should the field worker conduct the administration in nearby schools? A second example: A field worker in the same country found that a sample school in a mountainous region could not be reached because it was on the other side of a flooded river. Should the field worker wait for the flood to subside?

(b) *The field staff make on-site alterations to the sample design without seeking approval.* There are many temptations for the field worker, especially a poorly-paid one working in an isolated region of a country, to engage in "substitutions" whereby students, or even whole schools, are substituted for the students and schools in the "official sample design". These pressures are sometimes financial -- because the field workers are paid fees and per diems on the basis of an agreed number of schools, they are sometimes cultural -- because local custom makes it difficult to say "no" when a school principal or a regional official "suggests" that only the best students should be tested, and they are sometimes due to the field worker replacing the sample school with another school -- because the "replacement" school was more accessible.

It is extremely difficult to obtain complete protection against these kinds of actions. However, all data collections should attempt to include some form of "external validation" through either conducting a "post-enumeration survey" (Casley and Lury, 1981), or through including a few already-known pieces of information in the data collection (for example, class/school size, age of school principal, number of teachers, sex composition of school) and then later comparing these returns with official records. Unfortunately, these issues are often ignored or, at best, a half-hearted "internal validation" is conducted in which the researcher subjects a few of the completed questionnaires to a visual inspection in order to look for inconsistent patterns of response.

(c) *The Test Administrators accidentally give some of the respondents the wrong combination of instruments.* If the data collection instruments are complex due, for example, to the use of rotated forms, multi-matrix sampling, or balanced incomplete block item allocation, then confusion may result in some respondents receiving the wrong combination of instruments. Other problems that may arise when the instrumentation is complex include the following: errors made in time allowances for different test booklets, student control problems if one test booklet within a rotated group of tests takes about half the time to complete than has been planned for, student confusion if the Test Administrator does not read and understand the procedural requirements of the testing session before it has commenced.

(d) *The administrative procedures presented in the School Co-ordinator's Manual and Test Administrator's Manual are not subjected to a rigorous trial-test before being used in the field.* A data collection programme can be endangered if any confusion arises during the field work concerning the instructions given in either the School Co-ordinator's Manual or the Test Administrator's Manual. These manuals should be trial-tested in some settings where confusion is *most likely* to arise.

It is very difficult for a researcher, sitting in modern, air conditioned government offices in the nation's capital city, to write clear and concise instructions using a level of language that will suit all of the people involved in a data collection. Therefore, trial testing of all of the manuals should be carried out in a range of "difficult" environments that, for example, could include: isolated parts of a country where the Test Administrator may be required to fit in with unfamiliar local customs, or "urban ethnic enclaves" where the everyday language of the people may not be the same as the national language in which the manuals have been prepared, or primary schools in certain provinces where the language of the first years of schooling may be conducted in a local dialect.

(e) *The data collection date is set at an inappropriate time.* The researcher needs to be extremely careful about setting the date for the data collection because a bad choice of dates can sometimes lead to poor response rates or unreliable data. For example, the "school climate" at certain times of the school year may not be appropriate for a data collection to proceed (due to impending vacations, approaching examinations, etc.), or there may be certain times of the year when religious festivals, especially those that require fasting, are likely to affect the collection of data from students.

(f) *The researcher lacks local knowledge.* There are many different situations where a lack of local knowledge can interfere with the collection of accurate data. For example, a researcher, who was responsible for estimating school participation rates gathered data in three provinces of a country where Islam was the predominant religion without realizing that many students would be attending two schools (government in the morning and Islamic in the afternoon). The resulting "double counting" of students attending school provided estimated participation rates in some villages of 120 percent! All of the field work for this part of the project needed to be repeated using appropriate counting methods.

The management of the data preparation

The data preparation phase is concerned with the transformation of raw data obtained during the data collection phase into a form that is suitable for later analysis. There are two main steps involved in this: data coding and data entry. *Data coding* requires the allocation of numerical codes to each piece of information gathered during the data collection. Sometimes this allocation will be self-evident -- as in allocating a 1, 2, 3, or 4 to the first, second, etc. responses to a test item. At other times it will require a careful use of special tables of information -- as in allocating a score on a scale of "socio-economic status" for an open-ended response describing the occupation of a student's father. *Data entry* requires the transformation of all of these codes into a form that can be "read" by a computer.

The data preparation phase of the work can spoil efforts that have been made to ensure a well-executed data collection. This often occurs because many researchers tend to see data preparation as being unworthy of their full attention since it involves neither the practical challenges of data collection nor the intellectual stimulation that goes along with data analysis. The authors have participated in the "recovery" of several data collections that had initially failed because the researchers responsible for them held this kind of attitude. In each of these cases it was found that the recovery was very expensive in financial and manpower terms.

Data preparation: basic requirements

(a) *The coding team and their working environment.* The data coding should be conducted by a trained team under the careful supervision of an experienced person who understands the content and purposes of the data collection. This team should be given a quiet and comfortable room in which to work so that there is little likelihood that the "normal distractions" of office life will occur. (For example, telephones should be removed or silenced, excessive social chatter should be discouraged, and office traffic should be kept to a minimum.) The room should be furnished in a manner that permits the coders to work quietly without interrupting each other. (For example, each coder should have a table that is sufficiently large to facilitate the management of questionnaires, tests, and related coding documents, and there should be adequate shelving and storage areas for the completed instruments.)

(b) *The "Codebook".* The data coding should be carried out according to the instructions set out in a Codebook that has been prepared by the researcher for the coding team. The Codebook should include an accurate reproduction of the each of the questions and test items, a list of the answers that are possible for these, a list of the codes that are to be assigned to the possible answers, an explanation of the missing data codes that are to be used, information describing the scoring and re-coding that will take place on the computer (for example, when test scores are produced, or highly detailed classifications are "collapsed" into a smaller number of categories), and the location of each coded value after it has been entered into the computer data file. The Codebook should contain sufficient information to permit a person who has had no prior knowledge of the data collection to understand the meaning and origins of every numerical value stored in the computer data file.

(c) *The coding procedures*. The coding should commence with a rapid general edit of the questionnaires in order to check for any errors associated with obvious omissions or inconsistencies and, if possible, to correct these errors. For example, at this point it will be possible to identify whether there are any missing questionnaires and to check the reasons for this with the field staff. The next task is to select a sample of around 25 questionnaires that will be coded by all members of the coding team and also by the researcher. If there are any differences in codes allocated for particular questions these should be noted and made the subject for a rentable discussion so that the researcher and all members of the coding team reach agreement about the requirements of the task and also about any areas of the coding that may occasionally require a "second opinion". At this stage, the coding of the all of the questionnaires should commence and the supervisor of the coding team should be available to participate in the work, to answer questions, and to conduct quality control checks by inspecting samples of completed work. The supervisor should keep an accurate record of exactly which questionnaires have been coded by each member of the coding team so that it will be possible to find and correct questionnaires when quality control procedures reveal that a particular person is "error prone". The researcher should meet with the supervisor at the end of each day in order to discuss any problems and, from time to time, should participate in the coding in a enthusiastic manner that demonstrates to the coding team that their work is important and that the researcher cares a great deal about this aspect of the data preparation.

(d) *Data entry*. The data entry component of data preparation refers to the transformation of the information compiled at the coding stage into a form that can be "read" by a computer. This is normally achieved by entering the codes into a computer via a terminal or a personal computer. The persons carrying out the data entry usually work either from sheets of figures produced during the data coding or from the questionnaires and tests themselves in the case where these contain mostly "self-coded" responses. Generally there will be less errors if the data are entered directly from the questionnaires and tests because this reduces the chances of error related solely to transcribing, however this approach may increase the time required for the data entry because of the need to read from various page locations and different pages. In some cases it may be possible to employ optical scanning whereby the respondent enters responses onto a form that can be read directly into the computer. This more advanced approach needs to be used with care, especially when applying it with young children, because a certain amount of maturity and dexterity is required on the part of the respondent in order to handle these forms in a manner that does not diminish the validity of the responses.

Several guidelines should be observed during the data entry: all codes should preferably be numeric, each respondent should have a unique identification code that includes both the respondent's location (for example, country, state, province, district, school, class) and the associated sampling frame information (for example, domain, stratum, substratum, cluster), a clear distinction should be made concerning the various forms of non-response (for example, omitted, not present, not reached, etc.), the value zero should not be used to indicate non-response, a "check digit" should be inserted every 10 or 20 columns in order to permit a visual check of data alignment to be made rapidly from the print-out, and the data should be "double punched" or validated in some similar manner.

In ideal circumstances a specialist data editing programme should be used to monitor the data entry in "real time" by conducting pre-programmed logic checks on the data as they are entered. These checks are conducted by the computer and may be as simple as a basic range check or as sophisticated as a complex check for unlikely combinations of many codes.

(e) *Data cleaning*. The final part of the data entry is called data cleaning and it consists of running a series of preliminary analyses on the data in order to look for errors, omissions, etc., and then employing the results of these analyses to edit the original data file. These analyses should expose some or all of the following problems: differences between the number of cases on the computer file and the number of questionnaires, non-numeric codes, out-of-range errors, logical consistency irregularities, mismatches between data collected at different levels (for example, data may be available for a particular teacher but not for that teacher's students), and errors in the preparation of composite variables on the computer. As a "rule of thumb" no more than three sets of these preliminary analyses should be undertaken because the authors' experience shows that, provided a careful clerical examination is undertaken on the results of the analyses, further runs do not always justify the time and computer resources involved.

After three sets of computer runs, the data should be run through a "conditioning" programme that either sets the values of imperfect composite variables to missing data according to pre-specified rules (for example, assigns a value of "missing" to a total test score when more than ten percent of the items are missing) or creates an imputed value for an imperfect composite variable (for example, assigns the class mean score for a student who did not provide information about one of the variables that is to be included in a construct describing the socio-economic circumstances of the student's home background). There is no single correct way with which to deal with non-response and therefore the researcher's task is to "choose the method with the least disadvantages for a specific situation" (Kish, 1965: 558). It should be remembered in the treatment of missing values that "doing nothing about it" (for example, by excluding the missing responses from all calculations of sample means) usually requires the simple, but usually incorrect, assumption that the non-respondents are sufficiently similar to the respondents to justify ignoring them in the calculations.

The final task of the data cleaning work is to produce two copies of the data files in addition to the working file. One of these copies should be stored on-site for backup purposes or for use in transferring data between computers, the other copy should be stored in appropriate long-term, secure, off-site storage.

Data preparation: what often happens

(a) *The coding and data entry team is untrained, poorly supervised, and works in an inadequate environment.* The implications of this kind of situation are best described by reference to the authors' experience in trying to recover a dataset that had been prepared under very poor conditions for a national survey of Grade 9 students. The coding team hired for the survey consisted of young university undergraduates and they worked on the coding in very cramped conditions on bench tables that had been placed in the corridors of the Ministry of Education building. The team was given a minimal amount of training and little, or no, supervision. Their main task was to transcribe student responses to questionnaires and tests onto coding sheets and then to enter the data into a computer.

The coding team did not complain about their working conditions -- indeed the young males seemed to enjoy being confined in small and unsupervised working area along with their attractive female colleagues. The roar of conversation, occasional squeals of laughter, incessant corridor traffic, smiling faces, etc. showed that the team was having a very good time as they spent several months working their way through the tests and questionnaires associated with some five thousand students. When the coding and data entry was completed, the tests and questionnaires were bundled together in a rather haphazard fashion and sent off to storage in a government warehouse located ninety minutes drive away.

The researchers conducted no preliminary analyses in order to check the quality of the data preparation. Instead, with an extraordinary demonstration of courage they launched into the main analyses using huge amounts of expensive computer and programmer time in scoring, merging, and analysing. However, it wasn't very long before some of the findings set the danger bells ringing: the mean scores on the multiple choice tests were close to values that would be expected if all the students had guessed the answers, a number of variables that had four possible responses had many values in the range 5 to 9, strange student and school identification codes were appearing in large numbers and seemed to resist any attempts made by the researchers to use them for file merging purposes.

A decision was made to check the first 100 cases on the computer files by referring back to the questionnaires and tests. This took a little while to get started because the researchers had to first go back to the warehouse and then to find the correct questionnaires among the thousands of unsorted returns from students, teachers, and school principals that had been stored in over a hundred cardboard boxes. When the checking was finally completed it was discovered that the miscodes on some of the coding sheets were as high as 75 percent. In addition, a large number of errors were discovered to be associated with the data entry work. There were so many errors that the only solution was to start the whole coding and data entry operation again from the beginning.

(b) *The coding team scores the tests and scales by hand.* It is still quite common to see researchers directing their coding teams to add the item scores to obtain a total test score and then enter the total scores, not the item scores, into the computer file. This inevitably results in the unnecessary inclusion of an extra source of error into the data preparation. The authors have noted a number of instances of this approach in projects that were conducted under the direction of external "expert" consultants. In addition to introducing errors into the total test, this procedure prevents the researcher from being able to conduct item analyses so as to remove poor items, to check the suitability of item membership of subtests, and to use item characteristics to check the validity of the answer key for the test. Many people would find the last item mentioned here a little unusual. However, the authors' experience in both developed and developing countries has been that errors may be be found in answer keys through the use of item analyses in around one out of every four projects.

(c) *The coding team is given inadequate documentation.* It is important that the documentation given to the coding team covers all possible situations. That is, the members of the coding team should never be left to "work it out amongst themselves". An example of this occurred in a country in Europe where, instead of being given a standard table, the coding team was left to transform dates of birth into a variable referring to age in months. This variable was a key marker variable for the project and the many "out of range" values cast doubt not only upon the sampling procedures, but also prevented the use of the variable as an important control for student achievement scores.

(d) *The researcher fails to "fine-tune" the early stages of the coding operation.* During the first stages of the coding operation it is important to check the validity of the the Codebook with respect to the open-ended and free response items. It is often the case that the respondents will provide some answers that do not completely fit all of the possibilities that are listed in the Codebook. In some circumstances this will require further categories to be added, while in other cases it may require a complete rewrite of a section of the Codebook. These changes need to be made very quickly and this is yet another reason why the researcher needs to participate with the coding team in the early parts of the data preparation. An example from a project in Australia illustrates this with respect to the coding of occupations on a scale of occupational status. The coding manual for the project provided the coders with a table to be used to look up a "socio-economic status score" based on the question "What is the name of your fathers occupation?". The coders dutifully followed these instructions without taking advantage of the much more informative responses that the students had provided to a later question which asked "What does your father do when he is at work?". In a large number of cases, students received a "missing data" code because they had not responded to the first question or had written "I don't know". Nearly all of these students could have been assigned valid scores if responses to the later question had been taken into consideration by the coding team.

(e) *The data are "lost"*. The data collected for the project are often lost shortly after the researcher completes the project, and this prevents important secondary analyses from being undertaken. Some of the main reasons for losing the data are: the tapes and disks containing these data are stored carelessly and then simply "lost"; the principal researcher moves to another job and the project data are cleaned off the main computer's disks in order to make way for new data; the Codebook is either inadequate or non-existent and consequently when the principal researcher leaves nobody can remember what is in the computer data files; there are so many versions of the data files that it is impossible to know which data represent the "clean" files. The authors know of one country (that has a strong tradition for conducting well-designed, large-scale, and expensive national evaluation studies) in which only one of the datasets for the past four national testing programmes conducted for Grade 6 and 9 can be located.

Data analysis

The data analysis stage is mainly concerned with the preparation of usable summaries of the data that have been collected and prepared for analysis. These are usually, at least, in the form of descriptive statistics (for example, means, standard deviations) and cross tabulated frequency counts. In some cases there will be a need for significance tests (for example, "treatment versus control" comparisons), and/or tests of the fit of proposed models (for example, causal models based on path analyses). The data analyses for sample

surveys must be preceded by the researcher deciding upon the
sampling weights that are required, and then followed by the
researcher calculating appropriate measures of sampling error for
each estimated population parameter.

Throughout all of this work the temptation to allow the
computer to take control of the analyses must be resisted. To achieve
this, the researcher must "get his/her hands dirty with the data" by
selecting a small sub-sample of cases and using these to replicate
some of the computer analyses by hand. For example, using paper,
pencil, and calculator, some simple descriptive statistics and
frequency distributions should be prepared, "outliers" should be
examined in detail, and "unusual" combinations of scores should be
noted for further consideration.

The following discussion sets out the steps that should be
followed in order to set the stage for a successful analysis of the data.
No attempt has been made to advise upon the selection of particular
data analysis techniques because these must be selected to fit in with
the aims of the data collection and must also match the researcher's
capacity to manage and interpret results produced by these
techniques.

Data analysis: basic requirements

(a) *The reward structure.* The reward structure for data processors
is a key factor in obtaining, and keeping, a qualified and experienced
research team for one or more projects which may extend over
several years. Talented data processors are few in number and they
take a very long time to gain the kind of experience that is necessary
to manage complex data collections in the field of education. The
best way to keep these people interested in, and enthusiastic about, a
long-term project is to offer an attractive "package" of working
conditions and benefits which should include appropriate
remuneration, access to computing facilities that are suited to the task
at hand, and, in some cases, acknowledgement as a co-author of the
project report.

(b) *The computer output should be designed to fit the requirements
of the decision-makers before the data have been analysed.* The
general format of the computer output should be prepared in draft
form during the design of the data collection. That is, discussions

123

should be held at a very early stage with the planners at the appropriate decision-making levels of the education system in order to establish sets of dummy tables. These discussions should be held mainly with those persons who will *use the data -- for decision-making purposes*. Care should be taken to limit the participation of "arm-chair sociologists" at this time because, in the authors' experience, such persons tend, often in a well-meaning way, to confuse and side-track the discussion. An attempt should be made, before the data preparation stage has been completed, to use some hypothetical data to fill out the dummy tables by hand. The data processing staff should then use these data to reproduce the hand-made tables on the computer for inspection and approval by the educational planners.

(c) *The construction of test and sub-test scores.* The preparation of test scores and sub-test scores should be accompanied by appropriate reliability and validity information. At the most minimal level for norm-referenced tests, a traditional item analysis should be undertaken in order to check that the items are "behaving" in an acceptable manner with respect to discrimination, difficulty level, and distractor performance. The reliability of each test and sub-test should be calculated and an attempt should be made to establish the validity of these where this has not been carried out in other projects. If the reliability of a test or sub-test fails to meet an acceptable level then consideration should be given to removing the test or sub-test concerned from the analyses.

(d) *Sampling errors and sampling weights.* The sampling errors and sampling weights should be constructed with the assistance of a sampling statistician in situations where the sample design deviates from simple random sampling by including complexities such as stratification, multiple stages of selection, or clustering (Ross, 1985). The importance of using the correct procedures to calculate the sampling errors has been mentioned previously in this paper. It is important to remember that sampling weights are usually always required, even for so-called "self-weighting" sample designs, because of imperfections in the sampling frame and/or the need to correct for non-response.

(e) *The computing equipment.* The advent of relatively inexpensive and very high-powered modern micro-computers now means that, except perhaps for some extremely large data collections such as student-level censuses using many variables, it is possible for the researcher to do most of the data processing on micro-computers. This situation has a number of advantages over the use of a centralized mainframe computer: it reduces "turn around" time for the writing and testing of computer runs, it allows the researcher to conduct the data processing operations without the need to fit in with the needs of other computer users, it encourages the researcher to stay in "stay in touch with the data", it provides the flexibility to work at times and on days when central mainframe machines might not be operating, it facilitates the sharing of data in electronic form on diskettes or via modem using telephone lines.

While the use of a personal computer has many advantages, there is one important disadvantage: the researcher now becomes responsible for making security backups of important data files. The best way to manage these backup procedures is to employ a "streaming tape" system that can be used in association with software that automatically, at pre-specified times and dates, transfers important datasets from hard disk storage to tape.

(f) *The software.* As a minimum requirement, the researcher should have access to a copy of one of the main-stream statistical packages that are now available for both personal computers and mainframe computers. Two of the more widely-used examples of these are the SPSS and SAS packages. These packages provide almost all of the data management and data analysis procedures required to analyse most small or large data collections, they are very well-documented and, because of the continual testing of them by a wide community of users, they are comparatively "bug-free". These packages often also include data entry software that permits the researcher to design project-specific data entry routines.

If possible, one of these packages should be supplemented by a general purpose item analysis programme to be used for the investigation of test and item characteristics, a spreadsheet programme to be used for the construction and manipulation of tables of figures, a word processing programme to be used for report preparation, and a full-screen editing programme that will permit the perusal and editing of data sent to the researcher on diskette.

Data analysis: what often happens

(a) *The data processing is never completed satisfactorily.* There have been many data collections carried out in the field of education that have contributed very little because of a failure to complete the data processing to a satisfactory standard. In the worst cases, failure takes the form of the analysis terminating at a very preliminary stage with the researcher caught in a tangled, and expensive, mess that has lost contact with the data analysis needs of the educational planners who were originally perceived as the clients for the whole exercise.

The authors' observations suggest that this kind of failure is generally associated with one of the following three causes: a lack of basic training and experience with respect to managing computer-based data analyses, an over reliance the "authority" of computer print-out at the expense of some personal familiarity with the data, or a fascination with computing technology that leads the researcher to go on-and-on playing around with "computing gymnastics" without finding the time to produce the analyses needed to write the kind of report that is meaningful and accessible to educational planners.

In other situations, failure occurs because of the the reward structures that are are associated with the component of the project concerned with data analysis and report writing. The authors have observed a number of talented research workers who, when the field work stage of a project is completed turn their attention to lobbying for the next opportunity to obtain control of a project - preferably an "externally funded" project that is likely to have high per diem and allowance rates. The data processing is then left in the hands of poorly trained and inexperienced junior staff, or in some cases in the hands of external contractors, who have little real interest in the purposes or importance of the project. This results in the data analysis being conducted in a superficial manner that rarely meets the requirements of the original project objectives. There are a number of countries in the world where this kind of behaviour has become institutionalized to such an extent that a whole generation of researchers now consider it to be "a way of life".

(b) *The researcher lacks fundamental knowledge and experience concerning the application of basic statistical and psychometric procedures.* There are many researchers who have received some formal training in basic statistical and psychometric theory. However, this training is often presented in a way that fails to establish links between the theory and the kinds of "real" data analysis questions that they are confronted with in their own countries. This kind of training offers a broad, but mostly superficial, knowledge structure that bypasses the need for a solid grounding in *applied* scaling, estimation, and model building. The problem is best illustrated by listing some examples of the types of errors that occur constantly in published research reports.

- *Measurement Errors.* The researcher reported the mean, standard deviation, and number of items for the total scores on a test but claimed that the reliability could not be calculated because only total test scores, and not individual item-level information, were entered onto the computer file. In fact, the most commonly presented estimate of test reliability, Kuder-Richardson formula 21 (KR-21) may be calculated using a little arithmetic in association with the three statistics mentioned above. The authors calculated the values of KR-21, by hand, for two key criterion test scores used by the researcher and found them to be so low as to suggest that the validities of the tests, and the sweeping generalizations made about them, were questionable.

- *The interpretation of test scores.* The researcher reported the results of a testing programme in which tests in school subject areas were administered to a sample of respondents. For each test, the average of the percentage of correct items per respondent was calculated. The researcher then discussed differences in these values across the tests as if they had some clear linkage to hypothetical knowledge domains. In fact, they were merely an artefact of differences in test difficulty. This mistake is often observed in analysis of national examination scores, where "pass rates" are set arbitrarily to match available places at the next level of education. In one country, national statistics on primary level completion scores were reported at the same level for several years, and interpreted as an indicator of the stability of the education system's quality. In fact, the pass rates were arbitrarily set, so that the same fixed percentage of students passed the test each year.

- *Reporting "differences" in mean scores.* The researcher reported the mean scores for subgroups of a sample on a multiple choice test of Reading. Statements were made about "differences" in performance levels between the groups. These statements were presented without any information being provided concerning the standard deviation of the test scores, the sampling errors of the test scores, or the reliability of the test scores.

- *Opportunities for creating composite scores.* Te researcher gathered many variables describing the socio-economic circumstances of students' home backgrounds and then reported some of these as univariate frequency distributions or in cross tabulations. There was no attempt made at constructing and employing one or more composite scores that might have summarized what were obviously replicated measurements of an underlying indicator of "socio-economic status".

(c) *Poor quality computing equipment is purchased and then operated in an inappropriate environment.* There is always a temptation, when research budgets are limited, to purchase the cheapest possible copies or "clones" of mainstream computing equipment, and then to cut corners in terms of the infrastructure required to house these computers. These kinds of "savings" are always illusory -- especially when a research unit needs to work effectively with large bodies of data and to be able to complete jobs according to tight deadlines. In many countries these problems are exacerbated by temperature and humidity extremes that do not suit the operation of fragile electronic equipment, by unpredictable electrical power supplies, and also by difficulties in obtaining spare parts and service when breakdowns do occur.

The authors' experienced difficulties in this area while working to an extremely tight schedule on a very large project concerned with the quality of primary schooling in Asia. The data processing for the project was conducted in a building that had no air-conditioning to control the large fluctuations of temperature and humidity. At the end of three weeks of heavy usage, one of the four personal computers allocated for the project had broken down, two others had developed intermittent and unpredictable processing errors, and after one more week the fourth machine was giving occasional read-write errors on its hard disk drive.

(d) *The researchers lack training in the use of some of the data manipulation procedures associated with the main statistical software packages.* Many educational researchers can operate the main statistical software packages, such as SPSS and SAS, at an elementary level. However, they have had no training in how to use this software to conduct a number of important exercises in data manipulation: sorting, merging, disaggregation, aggregation, etc.

The result of a lack of knowledge in this area is that student, teacher, and school datasets, are often analysed separately at a superficial level without merging datasets in order to explore the inter-relationships between all sources of data. The analysis of separate data files prevents the researcher from exploring research questions "across" the different sources of data. For example: What are the relationships between student achievement levels and teacher knowledge of subject matter after controlling for home, school, and community factors that might influence the educational environment?

(e) *Observational data or open-ended responses.* In any situation where observational data and/or open-ended test questions are used it is essential that, at least for a part of the data, some attempt is made at calculating the inter-rater reliability coefficient. This coefficient sometimes may be used to reveal that an excessive level of subjectivity has entered the scoring procedures, or that the raters have scored the responses along different dimensions by applying different criteria during the scoring. If the inter-rater reliability is very low it means that there is little, or no, agreement between raters with respect to the scores that they allocate for any single response and/or observation.

Often a failure to carry out these important checks on the stability of ratings is due to complete ignorance on the part of the researcher rather than a reluctance to carry out the small amount of extra work that is required. An example of this occurred where the researcher went to the expense of having two persons assess each piece of writing before coming to a decision on the rating to be given. Unfortunately, the researcher never considered taking the extra step of using these pairs of ratings to obtain a reliability estimate.

What might be done in the future

This chapter has explored some of the issues and problems associated with the sampling, collection, preparation, and analysis of data designed to assist educational planners to make decisions aimed at improving the quality of education. For each of these four activities, a discussion of the "basic requirements" was placed alongside some examples of problems that the authors have observed -- in both developed and developing countries.

While these problems covered a broad spectrum, the root causes of most of them may be grouped under two broad headings:

> *A lack of training and experience in the application of basic research procedures to "real" data.*
> and,
> *A lack of training and experience in research management techniques.*

There is a need for international agencies to take the initiative by preparing training programmes in these two areas. It is important that these training programmes should be flexible (with respect to sequence and length of presentation), and also capable of being constantly updated (with respect to content). Therefore, the design of these programmes must include a continuous formative evaluation process based on various sources of information that might, for example, include interviews with graduates of the programme and/or critiques prepared by successful practitioners. The results of these investigations could be used to extend and improve the training materials and, in some cases, form part of the pedagogical development of the programme. For example, some of the project reports prepared by the graduating trainees might eventually be included as "case studies" within the materials provided for later groups of trainees.

In the following section, the authors have listed a set of "guidelines" that they have developed for themselves based on their own successful *and* disastrous attempts at presenting a range of training programmes. This is then followed by some proposals for a training programme that attempts to satisfy most of these guidelines.

Authors' guidelines for training programmes

(a)   Selecting and working with trainees

- Establish that the trainees are familiar with the language in which the training programme is to be presented.
- Select the trainees as "country teams" and ensure that all members of a team are actually working on the same, or a related, project.
- Ask each country team to appoint a "team leader" who will take responsibility for his/her team's overall behaviour and performance.
- Meet with, or at least speak with by telephone, the team leader's Senior Officer in order to explain fully the nature of the training programme, and also to reach agreement on the rights and responsibilities of each trainee. Confirm all of these matters in writing with this person.
- Avoid cultural, intellectual, and official blunders both within and across teams by becoming familiar with the following matters before the training commences: age and provincial origin (both very important in some parts of Asia and Africa), educational qualifications, previous research training/experience, status in terms of the "official hierarchy" (government rank) and the "unofficial hierarchy" (team rank).

(b)   Process and content of the training programme

- Teach theory only in a "learning by doing" mode that requires the trainees to apply the theory as part of a "real" project.
- Keep interest and motivation at high levels by having the trainees work on a project that is nominated as "high priority" by the government of their own country.
- At the design stage of the project ensure that hypotheses and propositions are prepared in a form that permits clear policy directives to be made after the hypotheses and propositions have been subjected to empirical test.
- Visit the trainees in their own countries during the field work stage in order to provide assistance and/or intercept any problems.

(c) Outcomes of the programme

- Obtain a clearance from the participating countries before the commencement of the programme that the project will result in "knowledge made public" -- probably in the form of, at least, a short published research report prepared by each country team.
- Hold at least one seminar in each participating country in order to draw out the policy implications of the project results.
- Help the trainees to prepare a computer-based data archive.

Some suggestions for a training programme

(a) Programme content

Basic research skills. Throughout this chapter it has been pointed out that the practical skills and knowledge required to deal effectively with the logistics associated with the sampling, collection, preparation, and analysis of data are essentially those required in order to conduct educational research. There are many textbooks on educational research methods - but these books generally offer very little assistance for an educational planner faced with a "real" project in education.

The setting up of the training programme should therefore commence with a preliminary review of the basic practical skills and knowledge that are required to carry out this kind of work. This review would establish a "blueprint" for the design of the training programme. Flexibility in adapting to the needs of trainees from different backgrounds could be achieved by preparing the programme in the form of "stand alone" modules that could be combined in a variety of sequences of varying lengths. In the first instance, modules should be prepared to cover the areas of sample design, indicator specification, test and scale construction, data preparation, data analysis and reporting.

Research management. Training materials in the research management area should be prepared using the same strategy and format described above. In the first instance, modules should cover the areas of research design (including operationalization of research questions and planning the utilization of project resources according to a project timetable), the management of fieldwork (including the construction of manuals for the Test Administrator and the School

Co-ordinator), the management of data coding teams and data entry teams, the development of data archives, the selection and management of computing equipment and software.

(b)   The format of the training.

The training programme should be centred around a "hands on" teaching approach in which the trainees would be expected to be already involved in, or about to be involved in, a project that requires the type of skills and knowledge addressed by the training programme. The training modules described above should be integrated with doing "real" projects nominated as "high priority" by the trainees' own countries.

The depth and scope of this training approach could not be covered in a "short course" of, say, two to four weeks. Such a course would not allow time for the trainees to apply their skills in a "learning by doing" mode. The length of the course should be arranged so as to be congruent with the the length of a reasonably substantial piece of educational research, say at least one year, and could be composed of the following four segments:-

- Two months in the home country engaged on pre-training tasks such as literature review, collecting statistics for sample design, etc.
- Three months outside the home country (or in a place far removed from the usual working environment) in order to plan the project, including the sample design and the development of specifications/first drafts for instrument construction.
- Six to eighteen months in the home country for instrument construction, trial testing, data collection, and data preparation.
- Three months outside the home country (or in a place far removed from the usual working environment) for data analysis and report writing.

The six to eighteen months spent in the home country could be supported by a visit from a member of the training team in order to review progress and, if necessary, arrange for any supplementary assistance that might be needed before the second three month training session.

(c) The selection of trainees

If the training programme is to be centred around the conduct of a project, it would be preferable for the trainees to be selected from among those persons who expect to be, or who already are, working on a project. Since these kinds of projects are usually worked on by a research team, it would be desirable for the training to be focused on "country teams" rather than individuals. That is, at least two persons from a research team in each participating country should attend the training programme. There are a range of supplementary benefits associated with a team approach to training. For example, a team approach provides a form of "insurance" against the project failing at the data collection stage (due to illness, job transfer, etc.), and it also gives the trainees a greater opportunity to discuss the ideas presented during the training in their own time and, in some cases, in their own language.

Conclusion

This chapter has highlighted some of the basic requirements, and some of the more common problems, associated with the sampling, collection, preparation, and analysis of data required by decision makers for planning the quality of education. It was argued that the majority of the problems that were described could be addressed by appropriate training programmes and, accordingly, some broad proposals were advanced concerning the design of one such programme. These proposals attempted to satisfy most of the "guidelines" that the authors had developed for themselves based on their own successful, and disastrous, experiences. It should go without saying that the detailed design and preparation of training programmes in this area will demand the active involvement of several potential clients so as to ensure that both the content and pedagogy of the programmes matches the requirements and learning styles of future trainees.

Chapter 7

Improving the dialogue between the producers and the consumers of educational information[1]

Introduction

This chapter addresses the issues of how information can be more effectively communicated to educational decision-makers -- from politicians in national governments to school principals, teachers, and parents. Effective communication generally requires the following two conditions to be satisfied. First, the decision-maker who is receiving the information must have previously asked a question, or at least have been presented with evidence that reveals a problem worthy of priority attention. Second, the decision-maker must have the opportunity to manipulate, interpret, and assign meaning to the information. The probability that a decision-maker will actually use information increases significantly when the evidence advances the decision-maker's interests and efficiency.

In short, providing evidence and data to an educational decision-maker represents communication only when the decision-maker is actively listening and reflecting on a related

---

1. This chapter was prepared by Bruce Fuller, Dorothy Gilford, Archie Lapointe, Abdel Ghani Al-Nouri and Etienne Brunswic.

problem. Otherwise, educational planners are presenting evidence and answers to an audience that may be asking unconnected questions. Simply communicating more information fails to address the need to harmonize the questions being asked by decision-makers with the evidence being provided.

This chapter argues that educational planners must go beyond simply transmitting evidence and findings. Instead, there must be a continuing dialogue and interplay between (a) the decision-maker who demands information and assigns priorities to competing problems, and (b) the educational planner or educational researcher who produces data and infers certain meanings from evidence. The structure of information demand -- and how issues are framed -- provide windows of opportunity through which the educational planner can have a significant impact on important educational policies.

Educational planners can boost their influence by adopting a proactive stance that aims to assist decision-makers to frame issues and questions in more technically sound ways. The main requirement of this approach is that the planner must grasp how "the problem" is being understood by the decision-maker, and then move outwards from this initial formulation by carefully illustrating how better questions can be asked of data.

This chapter first illustrates how more interesting and meaningful questions about educational inputs might be raised within central governments. Second, the structure of question-asking and "rationality" in education ministries is taken up, emphasizing the implications for educational planners struggling to communicate more effectively. Third, three forms of information demand exercised by policy makers or education managers are delineated. Fourth, concrete cases are presented where decision-makers have demanded information and planners have responded with varying degrees of effectiveness.

In most national education systems planners continue to apply traditional methods for disseminating information. For the most part, their general approach has been to work outside of the operational circles where most policy decisions are taken. The starting point for this chapter is the assertion that the educational planner must be intimately involved in the deliberations and organizational culture of the educational decision-maker at all levels of the system -- from the central ministry to local schools. That is, the planner needs to get closer to the action. Only then can new information provided by the planner harmonize with the decision-maker's own problems, constraints, and questions (Weiss, 1980).

Framing the important questions

The first step in this process requires the planner to achieve a better understanding of the types of questions being asked -- the basic structure of information demand. Different types of information demands require different types of problem statements, information users, forms of research, and communication strategies. The following discussion explores four different sources of information demand.

Central decision-makers have historically focussed on expanding and reinforcing standard forms of schooling. So, the questions asked by decision-makers at the national level commonly include: What are the current and projected enrolments? What are the future staffing requirements? At what rate are new schools and classrooms being built? Are teacher training colleges keeping-up with enrolment growth? How many textbooks and basic instructional materials are required by the schools?

The majority of management information gathered by education systems is usually aimed at addressing these fundamental descriptive issues. These data are useful in diagnosing problems related to the overall supply of school inputs, and whether the simple organizational structure of schooling is intact and expanding. However, this type of descriptive evidence tells us very little about the following facets of school inputs:

(a) Are inputs being *deployed efficiently* across different subsectors? For example: Should very high pupil/teacher ratios within primary schools be allowed to exist while there are low ratios within secondary schools?

(b) Are scarce resources being *allocated efficiently* among alternative inputs? For example: Should teacher training institutions emphasize training in subject matter areas or in teaching skills? Would it be better to do neither and instead invest in more textbooks?

(c) Are inputs *allocated equitably* among different groups of families and students? For example: Should per student spending on urban schools be greater than on rural schools? Are urban schools holding all the experienced and talented teachers because the communities associated with rural schools cannot afford to pay salary supplements?

(d) Are material inputs and human resources *utilized effectively* within schools and classrooms? For example: Have teachers failed to integrate new textbooks and equipment into their lessons? How do teachers integrate, or reject, new materials and methods as they organize the classroom?

If the ultimate goal of decision-makers and planners is to raise student achievement, these more critical questions about the supply, distribution, and mobilization of educational resources should be asked more frequently and more forcefully. But why are such issues raised so infrequently? Can planners improve the information they presently collect to both frame and respond to these deeper questions regarding school inputs? These latter issues are taken up in the following discussion and some propositions are put forward in an attempt to explain why there has historically been a major dislocation between the information resources produced by educational planners and the burning questions ever present in the minds of decision-makers.

Institutional obstacles to framing the important questions

Information that circulates in ministries of education -- including formal data communicated explicitly and beliefs reproduced implicitly within an organization's deeper culture -- signals actions and events that most worry the institution. The creation and communication of information, from data on where to build classrooms to information on teachers' real earnings, indicate problems and remedies that may receive priority attention. Why, then, do educational planners spend so much time collecting simple descriptive data on numbers of students, teachers, and classrooms -- largely ignoring deeper questions regarding how inputs are

distributed, mobilized by teachers, and then experienced by children
in the form of achievement gains?

Organizational incentives

When educational planners complain that their minister or
department director is not listening to technical information, they
commonly infer that the organization is not rational. Indeed,
communications regarding the equitable distribution, utilization, and
school-level effects of alternative inputs would be heard more
frequently if the decision-makers' form of rationality addressed these
issues. But high-level decision-makers are usually rewarded for
following a political logic, not by other forms of rationality that value
efficient allocation of resources, maximizing pedagogical
effectiveness, or ensuring equitable levels of school quality.

The state is most concerned with (a) expanding schooling and
signalling the spread of mass opportunity, and (b) demonstrating its
organizational capacity to provide classrooms, teachers and materials
that appear to have acceptable quality. The legitimacy of central
government declines sharply when school construction or enrolment
growth slows, teachers are in short supply, or parents discover that
their children are learning little in schools with few books, no paper,
no desks, or decaying classrooms. When the essential and visible
contours of the school's infrastructure begin to crack, the state's own
credibility comes into question (Fuller, 1990).

Decision-makers in education feel sharp incentives and swift
sanctions when they behave according to this form of political
rationality. Rewards are higher for those who can attend efficiently to
concrete symbols of school expansion and clear symbols of
educational quality.

Sometimes decision-makers move beyond those more immediate
problem areas and ask questions about the equity with which inputs
and subsidies are flowing; or whether new tin roofs on schools
actually relate to student achievement; or whether traditional teaching
practices undercut the learning effects of new textbooks. But this
requires ignoring the structure and incentives operating within the
political framework. So, these more penetrating questions are often
lost, swamped by the priority and steady information linked to the
primary agenda: expanding infrastructure and providing concrete
symbols of school quality. Educational planners may optimistically

produce papers and evidence on these deeper questions about inputs. But over time few organizational incentives encourage managers to listen, reflect, and act on the basis of this information.

Bounded rationality

A softer argument is that government policymakers and mid-level managers really are concerned with technical effectiveness -- in our case allocating scarce educational resources to effective inputs that boost student achievement. However, even when political imperatives and logic can be buffered, the nature of bureaucratic organization constrains the pursuit of technical rationality. Here the educational planner is not speaking to deaf ears. But the decision-makers find the communication of data unclear, overwhelming, or difficult to connect with operational improvements.

A large research literature has emerged in Europe and the United States articulating how the technical rationality of organizations is constrained or bounded (Simon, 1957; Scott, 1981). A portion of this work comes from researchers who ask: Why is the utilization of technical information so low in public policy circles and government bureaucracies? The following discussion has highlighted the most influential elements that bound the rationality of education ministries. These constraints must be respected, or overcome, when planners attempt to formulate and communicate issues and evidence.

(a) *Schools and teachers are pushed to serve a variety of competing objectives.* Yet the teacher works in isolation within the walls of the classroom. And both the school headmaster and the teacher employ an ambiguous technology in acting out the schools various instructional and social goals. At best, the local school is loosely-coupled to district education offices, provincial or national ministries. How to structure and communicate information that travels effectively across bureaucratic layers -- to influence school-level improvements is quite problematic. Educational organizations are best seen as a collection of mostly independent groups which, only occasionally, overlap and share information and opinions. Educational planners must therefore decide whether their purpose is to inform policymakers about macro allocational and organizational choices or whether their work aims to inform local levels, closer to the school and classroom (Meyer and Rowan, 1977).

(b) *Politicians act upon some information and ignore other data.*
Information is optimal when it fits a politician's beliefs or the
interests of vocal interest groups. Educational planners must become
more skilled at communicating information that moves with the flow
of civic or political dialogue. The danger here, of course, is that the
analyst may at times be required to compromise technical standards
regarding the reporting of evidence.

(c) *Educational managers often are distracted by pressures from
outside their immediate organization.* Decision-makers at the
national level spend a considerable amount of time arguing with their
finance ministry for additional resources, or with other external
personnel and local government ministries over administrative
matters (Pfeffer and Salanck, 1978). Educational planners working
on school quality and efficiency issues should assess how to
capitalize on pressures generated by these external sources. Often,
interest groups outside ministries can construct a persuasive
campaign for reform when provided with appropriate technical
information.

(d) *Some information is more concrete and salient than other
data.* Education ministers frequently cite a problem that became
apparent when they visited a particular school: lack of desks, thatch
roofs falling-in, lack of parental involvement. These vivid stories
often carry more weight than careful, yet boring, technical analyses.
Skilled planners often use concrete cases, pictures, charts, and visual
presentations to sharpen images that are consistent with empirical
findings. In many countries, decision-makers are embedded in an oral
culture, and therefore if the planner has to write a memo to get the
decision-maker's attention then he or she reveals that the issue is
located outside the informal network surrounding the decision-maker.

(e) *Bureaucracy is held together by behavioural scripts,
standard procedures, and ritualistic action -- not by a flow of well
reasoned and technically informed choices.* When new incremental
resources are given to the education ministry, the largest share
usually goes toward hiring additional teachers or raising pay through
the traditional salary structure. That is, informed "choices" are rarely
made regarding the deployment of supplementary resources. The
flow of these extra resources simply moves according to an

organizational script (Weick, 1976). Educational planners may argue wisely that a slice of this incremental funding increase should be used for instructional materials, or for more performance-related teacher incentives. But any suggested departure from the ritualized pattern is often seen as "too difficult", or "too risky", or a silly idea put forward by "the unrealistic planners".

(f) *Knowledge creep through the system may be more influential than attempts to force major policy changes.* We often assume that technical information goes to a benevolent dictator who "makes policy". But in reality policy, budget allocations, and incremental management decisions unfold more like a slow-moving river which occasionally shifts direction, slows and stagnates, or, in the political rainy season, moves with surprising speed and force. Educational planners should think more carefully about whether their communication is targeted to influence a discrete and clear decision, or whether they are trying to change the framing and priority placed on a specific issue over time (Weiss, 1980).

(g) *The ministry's reflective and critical capacity may be isolated within the bureaucracy.* The organizational separation of operational offices from the planning department is quite curious but very common in many education systems. Some ministries have emphasized this split by creating separate offices for long-term planning versus short-term strategic planning. This process has reduced incentives for operational managers to think constructively about how to improve their particular programmes because, unless the planning office is called in to evaluate implementation, standard operational procedures will be viewed as satisfactory.

Alternative structures of information demand

The remaining parts of this chapter present examples of how management-related information is (a) *demanded* by decision-makers, (b) *produced* by educational planners and researchers, either reacting to questions or proactively advanced to encourage action on formulated issues, and (c) *communicated* across various levels of the education system, organized interest groups, and the broader public.

First, we specify *three basic types of information demand*
which, in turn, drive the type of evidence that is generated and the
methods of communication that are more likely be effective.

Type 1: High level decision-makers may request information
that will inform discrete choices related to budget allocations, the
basic structure of local schools, enactment of special interventions, or
roles governing personnel. Here, information must be mobilized
quickly if it is to influence particular decisions. Example 1 presented
below reviews a specific case from the national education ministry in
the United States.

Type 2: Decision-makers in education system draw on
information frequently as they take a variety of allocation,
implementation, and administrative actions. In Example 2 three
illustrations have been presented -- from India, Malawi, and Qatar -
showing how mid-level managers' use of information sometimes
leads to major policy action. Managers also can change what formal
information is legitimated and collected within local schools - which
may lead to behavioural change.

Type 3: Educational planners can proactively develop and
communicate evidence in ways that frame and define how an issue is
debated. Clear and vivid evidence of a problem, for example low or
declining student achievement, can lead political leaders to assign
higher priority to the issue. Educational planners can then inform
decision-makers on how the problem can be more carefully
diagnosed and addressed. Here the planners play more of a leading
role in highlighting and defining "the problem" than they do in
designing remedies. In Example 3 an account is given of how
educational researchers can proactively energize the discussion of
low student achievement.

These three types of information demand define the boundaries
within which educational planners can work. First, each type of
demand leads to the articulation of different problem statements and
questions. Second, the type of demand implies participation of
decision-makers operating within different levels of the ministry or
local schools. For example, certain demand situations require the
planner to communicate with broader audiences and certain issues

lead to questions about the authority, social roles, and tools employed by bureaucrats or school-level staff. Third, the different demand situations suggest different forms of inquiry -- from drawing on available survey data, to original research, to case studies or in-depth ethnographic studies within schools and classrooms. Fourth, differences in information demand suggest different communication strategies, depending on audiences effected, problems uncovered, and levels of the education organization that must be moved if the issue is to be addressed. Each of the examples presented below touches upon these four areas which are bounded by each of the three types of information demand.

Example 1: Decision-makers demand information for a particular purpose

To provide a more detailed discussion of the process of responding to a policy maker's request, let us consider the question, "What do we know about the education of American Indians?", which was posed by a top United States policymaker several years ago. Because of the comprehensiveness of this question, the statistical officer responsible for assisting the policy-makers immediately attempted to focus the question, and to explore the utility of available data bases to address the issue, by posing a series of questions.

"Are you interested in the number enrolled in elementary, secondary and higher education? The number who complete school, their educational attainment? The number who receive a BA or a Ph.D? The percentage of the school-age population in school? The number who are teachers? Do you want this information compared with other ethnic groups, by region or state, by sex?" The answer to *every* question was "Yes". The policy maker was looking for all of the information available in order to be able to respond to questions likely to be raised as part of a government debate during the following week.

The statistical office began to explore the availability of data and to prepare tabulations. Although a fast-response system was in existence, it could not be used because of the one-week time limit. Core surveys provided recent data by state on enrolment in elementary and secondary public schools by ethnic groups. Corresponding data for private schools was not available. Another category of schools consisted of schools on reservations, which were administered by the Bureau of American Indian Affairs in the Department of the Interior. That bureau provided enrolment data for elementary and secondary schools on the reservations. Higher education surveys provided trend data on enrolments and degrees earned by ethnic groups. A survey of doctorate recipients conducted by the National Research Council contained information by ethnic group and field of degree. The Census Bureau had data on the size of the school-age population by ethnic group. It was therefore possible to tabulate the percentage of the school-age population in public schools by ethnic group, and the percentage of the school-age American Indians in Bureau of Indian Affairs schools.

Since private school enrolment data for American Indians were not available it was not possible to compute the percentage of the school-age population enrolled in private schools or the percentage enrolled in school (public, private, and reservation). These missing data were of some concern since religious organizations had established several private schools specifically for American Indian students.

The National Assessment of Education Progress Project, generally a major source of achievement data, did not have data for American Indians due to complications associated with sampling very small minority groups. Enrolment data by state and region were available but most of the American Indian population was concentrated in five states so data were tabulated only for these states and a group of "all other states". Data by sex were available. Information on special problems in educating American Indians was not available, but because of the concentration of the population in 5 states, telephone calls to the five state officers of education elicited a list of problems and provided good, although not complete coverage, for public education.

Example 2: Decision-makers demand information on the quality of education

In the following discussion three brief examples have been presented of how education managers -- at various decision-making levels -- demand information on the quality of education. These cases from developing countries focus on, in some cases, the capacity of educational planners to produce evidence, communicate these data, and help legitimate innovative actions linked to school improvement.

(a) *India.* In the mid-1980s, ministry officials began drawing together data describing the quality of education in primary schools. Although this level of education had been the responsibility of state governments, central ministry managers had grown increasingly concerned over signs that certain educational inputs which clearly formed essential pre-conditions for effective learning had not been provided for all schools.

A careful analysis of the All India Education Survey vividly illustrated the problem: fifty percent of all primary schools had no permanent classroom or building; thirty-five percent had just one teacher for all five grade levels; forty percent had no blackboards. In addition, many schools had no latrines, no access to clean drinking water, and no desks or chairs. That is, it was clearly self-evident that gains in student achievement could not be expected to occur unless these basic conditions were attended to satisfactorily.

These data fueled a debate within the national government over whether increased financial backing was required to ensure that these minimal school inputs were provided. In 1987, the national government initiated a US$ one billion initiative entitled "Operation Blackboard". This scheme provided grants to state governments for the purposes of adding one classroom and one new teacher to single-teacher schools (totalling over 600,000 schools in 1987), and to provide a package of essential basic teaching materials (blackboard, chalk, paper, books), mats for children to sit on, and simple furniture for teachers.

In the wake of this programme, three additional questions were put to the decision-makers operating at the state level. The first was concerned with the need to monitor, in a simple descriptive manner, the allocation of these supplementary resources to schools. For instance, one state found that most one-teacher schools had enrolments of under 10 children. In this state, adding a second teacher would be costly and inefficient. Second, national and state governments wanted to ensure that these new educational inputs were reaching the schools that had the lowest standard of provision. This was checked by collecting monitoring data on a sample survey basis. Third, some education managers asked whether the package of inputs provided under Operation Blackboard actually resulted in an increase in student literacy levels, and whether certain other inputs might be more effective.

Clearly the political will expressed by the Indian government was a key ingredient for this effort. However, it was only the collection of suitable descriptive information that helped to illustrate and monitor the dimensions of the problems associated with access to essential preconditions for learning. It is expected that, at a later date, the national ministry will arrange to gather evidence in order to establish whether this programme has actually boosted literacy levels among students.

The national ministry and state education officials are the major decision-makers in Operation Blackboard. The availability of descriptive information on the coverage of the programme motivated them to produce and deliver the required inputs, and also to emphasize greater equity in the distribution of resources. Information was not gathered from school principals, teachers, and parents regarding their perceptions of the effects of the programme. Their voices also need to be heard because this will encourage a more systematic debate concerning the evaluation and selection of inputs that are most likely to improve the quality of education.

(b) *Malawi.* The Malawi Institute of Education recently began to train district inspectors and headmasters on how they might observe teachers in the classroom. A simple observation instrument was designed, working from the research literature on teacher effectiveness. The inspectors were required to spend two summers and two short holiday periods at the Institute participating in in-service training courses that included work on identifying good and bad pedagogical practices. The training included extensive discussion concerning key questions such as: Should the local manager supervise and perform purely administrative tasks? Or should inspectors and headmasters encourage and demonstrate more innovative and effective teaching methods?

Interviews conducted at four different district education offices revealed that the inspectors had in fact changed their role, spending more time in the classroom, and using the modest classroom observation tool described above to provide feedback to teachers. Some of the features of this new role for inspectors were found wanting in terms of their "fit" to the Malawian social context. For example, inspectors' feedback was sometimes unclear or not helpful;

and teachers were confused to discover that the inspectors were now more concerned with their behaviour as teachers than they were with missing classroom windows. The fascinating part of this changed relationship between the inspectors and the teachers was that a modification in the information and tools employed by inspectors has resulted in a new level of professional and social interaction focussed on improving the quality of education. The questions asked by both inspectors and local education managers have moved towards the ways in which material inputs and human resources may be mobilized within the classroom in order to create gains in student learning outcomes. A very important benefit of this changed situation has been that information gathered by the inspectors is being seen more as a shared approach to problem solving rather than a regulatory requirement.

(c) *Qatar.* The problem of poor teaching skills can be given a very high priority when several government ministers place it high on their agenda. This occurred in Qatar in the late 1980s when the deputy-minister's programme evaluation committee took up the issue. The committee included mid-level ministry managers, educational planners, and teacher training representatives. The committee members were "hand-picked" to provide a suitable knowledge and organizational base from which questions and proposals could be developed and put forward to decision-makers.

Initially, a fact-finding mission was undertaken by an educational planner from the ministry who was also a member of the evaluation committee. Systematic interviews were held with school headmasters, teachers, inspectors, and teacher trainees. Many felt that pre-service training (lasting 4 years after senior secondary school) emphasized instruction in curricular content but inadequately addressed alternative pedagogical methods and ways of motivating pupils.

The resulting policy decision was to increase and more fully integrate the practice teaching for trainees. As a result, it was decided to have all teacher trainees spend one full day per week in real classrooms at the beginning of their third year of training. In-service training programmes were also reviewed in order to re-assess the teaching of pedagogical strategies.

This example demonstrated that when high-level political or bureaucratic decision-makers placed high priority on an issue it can often become more salient. Middle-level managers operating in this climate immediately see incentives for assertively asking questions, reviewing information and tackling remedies related to the highly legitimated issue. Also, in this situation educational planners gain political visibility and authority by mobilizing relevant information and tools which help define the problem and point to remedies that are more likely to be effective.

Example 3: Educational planners and researchers adopt a proactive stance by framing issues and generating information demand

The United States National Assessment of Education Progress (NAEP) offers a fascinating case of how educational planners and researchers can proactively begin to respond to pressing educational issues and thereby frame and refine the questions being asked. NAEP operates within the Educational Testing Service (a non-governmental educational research and development institution).

In the United States, there has been considerable discussion and debate at various decision-making levels concerning a variety of questions about student achievement levels. These questions have included: How much are students in the United States actually learning? How many young people are finishing or leaving school without gaining basic literacy skills? Why do students in the United States perform less well than their peers in other developed countries in the basic skill areas? What school inputs, human resources, and organisational strategies explain variation in the performance of students? These important questions have been raised vocally by parents, business groups, the media, and even teachers. This, in turn, has sparked interest among political leaders, adding force to these questions and bolstering demand for information which offers possible answers.

In considering these questions and issues, NAEP decided in 1983 that it would no longer consider itself a testing programme, a data collection project, or a research project. Rather it would consider itself "an information system". It also decided to be pro-active in disseminating results rather than to simply respond passively to questions. This suddenly meant that instead of considering initially what kinds of questions, cognitive and background, to ask of students and teachers, NAEP began each assessment phase by thinking about the kinds of reports that would be issued and what they should contain. In the first instance, a considerable amount of time and energy was devoted towards defining the audiences for NAEP reports. NAEP then asked: What questions would these audiences like to have addressed? What level of detail would they want or tolerate? What kinds of graphic descriptions in the publications would be expected to capture their attention? How should the data be presented in order to communicate the findings in a clear and meaningful fashion. Finally, how could the data be presented in ways that would minimize the chances of its being misused or misinterpreted? This new orientation meant that NAEP would become first and foremost an information system, and that a new data gathering effort would be required to be based on an innovative but sound research design.

During the planning of the project the area of information dissemination received the highest priority - even though it was less sophisticated than the technical design of the project and less costly than data collection or data analysis. This approach has led many people to say that the most sophisticated thing NAEP does is concerned with the project's technical design, the most expensive thing NAEP does is data collection, the most complicated thing NAEP does is data analysis, *but* the only thing NAEP does that makes a difference is the publication and dissemination of its findings!

The NAEP research team decided that the "policy makers" for education in the United States during the late 1980's were the members of the general public. That is, in order to affect policy it was acknowledged that it would be necessary for NAEP results to have an impact upon public opinion. In the United States the best way to achieve this kind of impact is to work through the mass media and accordingly (a) a newspaper writer was appointed to the research team with responsibility for ensuring that NAEP reports would be written so that lay people could read them, (b) advertising experts were engaged in order to assist with the production of NAEP reports that were visually attractive and based on casily-understood graphs and charts, and (c) NAEP reports were launched at national press conferences in association with material that made the media's task of reporting the research results much easier (in the form of attractively presented short press releases and written statements about the results prepared by nationally famous experts).

150

The result of this campaign has been that NAEP results are regularly featured in all important newspapers in the country, often discussed on national television, and periodically debated in weekly news magazines. This has caused a major increase in the interest level associated with NAEP results among decision-makers who had previously given only occasional attention to measured levels of educational outcomes. For example (a) school system administrators, school principals, teachers and parents constantly call and/or write to obtain NAEP reports, (b) politicians, especially State Governors, are highly motivated to "keep up to date" with new NAEP information releases, and (c) various business, political, and "pressure" groups that exert a great deal of influence on education systems regularly make NAEP results and research staff the focal points of their gatherings. At the school level, particular efforts have been made to include all school principals and teachers in the discussion of NAEP results by providing school principals with a "script" for a professional discussion of the results that includes suggested questions based on the data, and information that permits each school to compare itself with national statistics.

The steady flow of NAEP information to decision-makers at *all* levels of the education system in the United States has led to debates about the quality of educational outcomes being conducted on the basis of clear evidence rather than speculation. For example, the NAEP data have demonstrated a general improvement in Reading performance for students at three age levels in the period 1971 to 1984 (NAEP, 1986). At the same time there has been a decline in Science performance and this finding has resulted in pressures to review the school science curriculum. Other NAEP data demonstrate a dramatic improvement over the years in the performance of various ethnic groups, thereby providing evidence of the success of anti-discriminatory social policies adopted in the United States since the 1960's.

Conclusion

This chapter has put forward arguments that demonstrate that there is a need in each country to study the ways in which educational information resources may be linked to the questions that are foremost in the minds of decision-makers operating at various decision-making levels of education systems. Education is often one of the largest enterprises operating in a country and the circulation of useful information within an education system is of paramount importance if improvements in the quality of education are to be made on the basis of informed debate.

Special problems in this area often arise in situations where educational planners and decision-makers form separate communities that differ as to their views on education and the changes that are required to improve the quality of education. In summary, the communication breakdowns between these two groups may be traced to certain general characteristics of the groups.

Educational planners have often tended to be inflexible in the manner in which they have produced and disseminated information in the form of documents and publications. Their information reporting approaches are rarely addressed to the end-user. They often have difficulty in presenting a concise statement of the conclusions reached and the associated administrative changes that are required in order to improve the quality of education. They do not have the necessary skills or experience to help decision-makers to define and formulate their needs.

Decision-maker's interests have generally been linked to the present at the expense of a more serious consideration of the future prospects of education. They are more inclined to frame questions surrounding the visible aspects of school provision than about the comparative effects that various provisions have on educational outcomes. They often lack the skills required to properly interpret research outcomes or to discriminate between well and poorly designed and executed research studies.

Some of the difficulties arising from this communication breakdown could be addressed by extending the training of educational planners to include the development of skills in the following two areas.

(a) *The operationalization of important policy questions.* Skills in this area are required in order to assist decision-makers to improve and articulate their questions in terms that can be tested by research. In particular, there is a need for training in the documentation of such questions in a manner that will guide the assembly of evidence that is likely to provide clear conclusions and meaningful policy directives; and

(b) *The gathering and synthesis of research evidence.* Skills in this area are required in order to be able to gather evidence that addresses the decision-makers questions by (i) conducting highly focussed surveys that provide information specific to important questions of policy, and (ii) undertaking research syntheses (*not research abstracts*) in the form of, for example, meta-analyses and policy-related literature reviews.

An essential adjunct to more specialized training of educational planners would be a complete re-think of the traditional modes of information dissemination within education systems, and also between education systems and the surrounding world. The majority of educational planners are trained in the communication "genres" of academia. These forms of communication are often impenetrable for decision-makers because they are too long, too complicated, and in most instances, the conclusions are so loaded with caveats and cautions that the reader is unable to extract clear policy directives from them.

The kind of radical review of dissemination procedures described here cannot proceed by using a little re-training for educational planners and/or decision-makers. What is required are new approaches to bridging the gaps that exist between information provision and improvements in the quality of education. These approaches would include (a) the participation of groups that have had little to do with education systems in the past, for example, professional journalists, image-makers, media specialists, (b) the "opening-up" of education systems for more intensive participation by the community -- both as participants in the framing of policy-related questions *and* as providers of various kinds of assistance when fresh policy directives are put into place, and (c) the use of broadly-based public meetings, open-days in schools and other educational institutions, and print/electronic media, to air the issues, problems, and questions that decision-makers operating at *all* levels of an education system need to address.

Conclusion

Chapter 8

Fundamental research and training needs: an agenda for international action[1]

Educational planning has traditionally concentrated on matters concerned with educational inputs and student enrolments. However, since the mid-1970s governments have placed more and more emphasis on the quality of educational outcomes -- particularly the acquisition by students of higher levels of knowledge and skills. This change in focus has brought with it an increasing demand for more information about educational outcomes, especially in terms of student achievement in the core school subjects, and about the factors associated with the home, the neighbourhood, the school, and the teaching-learning process that affect student achievement.

The increased general demand for information has included specific requests by parents, school teachers, school principals, provincial and state officials, and national officials in ministries of education who want to know more about student achievement, and the factors that affect it, at the level of the education system (that is, student, class, school, province/state, nation) for which they are responsible. One of the problems associated with attending to these enquiries is that it is not always the same factors that affect student achievement for all decision-making levels, for all subjects, for all age groups, for all regions of a country, or for all countries. This

---

1. This chapter was prepared by T. Neville Postlethwaite, Jacques Hallak, and Kenneth Ross.

makes the task of educational researchers and planners extremely complex as they seek to provide evidence to decision-makers in a form that has clear implications for informed policy development and insightful policy change.

These difficulties are compounded in many countries because "objective" information about education may have less impact on decision-making than other political pressure groups or the personal preferences of influential persons. That is, the availability of information in itself -- even accurate, timely, important information -- provides no guarantee that it will always be taken into account when decisions are taken concerning the quality of education. With these cautionary points in mind, it is still true to say that most education systems around the world are placing a great deal of importance on the improvement of the quality of education through better decision-making based on the establishment of extensive educational information systems.

The discussion presented in each chapter of this book was centred around an acknowledgement that different kinds of decisions about the quality of education were made at different decision-making levels of an education system and that information requirements and appropriate modes of information communication also varied across these levels. Throughout the discussion there was mention of certain fundamental needs that had to be satisfied if educational planners were to be able to provide the kind of information that was essential for informed decision-making. These needs contained many common elements and it was possible to group them together under six main headings in order to consider the ways in which they might be addressed satisfactorily. In the following sections of this chapter the six main areas of need have been listed and then some proposals for developing appropriate responses to these needs have been presented.

Fundamental needs

1. The need for a complete reconceptualization of what information should be collected in order to assist with planning the quality of education.

Many ministries of education around the world collect information on the same set of indicators, often on a yearly basis using a complete census of schools, but without thinking through whether such data are still useful. A common justification for this approach is :"That's the way we have always done it!". In these ministries there needs to be a comprehensive review, at each decision-making level, of what data are collected, with what frequency, and for what purposes. As part of this review, an investigation needs to be undertaken to find out (a) which data are actually being *used* by decision makers -- as distinct from data that are collected, summarized, and published in a series of seldom consulted statistical yearbooks, and (b) which key questions associated with planning the quality of education do decision-makers require information about.

The nature of the educational enterprise is such that there is rarely one cause for a particular phenomenon. Multi-factor causation is the rule and not the exception. Therefore some wide-ranging decisions taken to reform an aspect of an education system will require the participation of several administrative units at several decision-making levels . The educational planner therefore needs to think carefully about the content, format, and delivery of information that is required for the various administrative units and decision-making levels. In order to establish exactly what is required, it will be necessary for the educational planner to be "receptive" to the expressed information requirements of decision-makers and, at the same time, to be "pro-active" in seeking to assist decision makers to articulate other information requirements that may provide them with more useful guidance.

2. The need to address several major gaps in most educational information systems that have been designed to assist with planning the quality of education.

While many ministries of education collect too much information that they do not use, there are several important items of information that are usually neglected. These are: student achievement levels (based on sound measurement principles and instrumentation), teacher subject matter knowledge, student time and tracking (based on time spent in contact with specific curricular objectives and on the levels and types of curricular options), and detailed cost information. These gaps present major barriers to conducting informed educational planning because they prevent the establishment and study of linkages between the levels and costs of various forms of educational provision and important educational outcomes. In the harsh economic conditions likely to be experienced by many countries in the 1990's, these linkages will become increasingly important because governments will be asking educational planners to provide optional scenarios for educational reform to be presented in association with evidence for both their effectiveness and their implementation costs.

3. The need to ensure that an educational information system, especially one that includes student achievement scores, delivers information to decision-makers that is (i) reported at the appropriate aggregation level (student, class, school, provincial/state, nation), (ii) reported at the appropriate scaling level (item, sub-test, total test), and (iii) gathered at the appropriate coverage level (sample survey, census).

In the following paragraphs some examples have been presented to illustrate what is implied by aggregation, scaling, and coverage. These illustrations do not exhaust the many situations where care needs to be exercised in the preparation of information that can be used by decision makers.

Aggregation. For example, teachers need to have detailed information about the achievement levels for each of their students in order to direct particular attention towards students that are experiencing difficulties. At the other extreme, national officials are not interested in the performance of individual students, classes, or schools. The national officials are primarily interested in differences in achievement levels among large groups of schools, such as provinces, and the broad policy-related factors that might be associated with such differences.

Scaling. As described above, teachers are interested in the performance of individual students. But it is also important to note that this interest is focussed on student performance with respect to *particular* items or clusters of items assessing specific performance dimensions. Information at this level of scaling provides an opportunity to review and revise particular aspects of the teaching-learning process (time spent on learning, deployment of teaching materials and aids, sequence and speed of instruction) for specific parts of the curriculum where student performance was not satisfactory. On the other hand, the national official is more interested in the broad patterns associated with overall total test scores -- especially for the "high profile" core areas of the curriculum such as Mathematics, Science and Mother Tongue Language. National officials need to make broad decisions about general performance levels across the whole or large parts of an education system so that long-term and expensive plans for major educational reform (such as major changes in curriculum, teacher training, equipment provision) can be implemented in a timely and orderly fashion.

Coverage. For example, at the national level in many countries, most of the policy-related decisions are not focussed on individual schools. Therefore, at this level a well-designed sample survey approach would suffice because there are very few pieces of information that are required to be collected from a complete census of schools. In contrast, for decisions taken at the school district level, information is required to be based on a complete census of all schools in the district because of the school-specific nature of decisions taken at this level.

4. The need to develop a meaningful two-way dialogue between information providers (educational planners) and information users (decision-makers operating at all levels of an education system).

In many countries there is a lack of meaningful dialogue between educational planners and decision-makers with respect to matters associated with the quality of education. This is not necessarily to say that the two parties have not tried hard enough to communicate, but rather that there are some features of bureaucratic organizations in which they work that often constrain the pursuit of technical rationality. In other words, the educational planner is not necessarily speaking to deaf ears, but rather he/she is often providing information that the decision-maker finds unclear, overwhelming, or difficult to operationalize in policy terms.

In order for improvements to be made in this area, a great deal more attention should be given to the need for educational planners and decision-makers to share in the formulation of questions pertaining to the quality of education. That is, the starting point should be to establish questions in a form that ensures that (a) the decision-maker knows that an answer to the question will be framed in a way that will provide direct and clear guidance for decision-making, and (b) the educational planner knows that the question is framed in a form that includes agreed operational definitions of the information that is required. As agreed questions are established, the educational planner needs to adopt a pro-active stance that includes anticipating information requirements, developing *useful* syntheses of research evidence, and exploring innovative techniques for "getting the message across".

5. The need to ensure high technical standards for the collection, preparation, and analysis of data required for planning the quality of education.

In many countries there is a great deal of information prepared using very poor data collection, preparation, and analysis procedures. When this occurs, all efforts put into the conceptual design of an educational information system are wasted because the results of the data analyses are meaningless, or the results are presented in a form

162

that is not useful for decision-makers, or the results are delivered far too late to be employed for decision-making.

Surprisingly, there are very few sources of information available that describe, in a systematic manner, how to move step-by-step through the fundamental procedures of a "real" data collection, preparation, and analysis project for an education information system. This is especially the case for moderate to large-scale data collection exercises. There is a need to document these procedures in a form that will be accessible to educational planners. This means that the procedures should be presented in a context that integrates theoretical and practical aspects with examples based on "real" projects.

6. The need to establish an international network of educational planners that will facilitate the sharing of knowledge and experience concerning the best approaches to planning the quality of education.

Many countries, developed and developing, share similar concerns about matters related to the quality of education. For example, many countries are striving to improve the overall achievement levels of their students, to increase the educational achievement of special subgroups of students (for example, female, rural, ethnic minorities), and to enhance the standards of teaching in mathematics and science. While these problems are common concerns, the ways in which they are addressed by different countries vary a great deal. In many ways, variation in steps taken by countries to solve these problems provides an important form of educational experimentation that all educational planners should seek to learn from. Unfortunately, at present, very few countries take the opportunity to learn from each other -- except perhaps in non-systematic ways such as individual study tours.

A key argument in support of attempts to improve international co-operation and information sharing in education is to be found in the field of curriculum development. There are many national curriculum development centres around the world, and even more curriculum units working within national, state, and provincial branches of education ministries. The work carried out by these centres and units is an expensive and time-consuming activity that would undoubtedly benefit through the sharing of knowledge between countries in terms of approaches that are known to provide both successful and unsuccessful curriculum materials and programs. It is the avoidance of major failures that is very important here because bad curriculum materials and programs can be extremely damaging to the long-term cognitive and affective development of whole cohorts of children.

The existing mechanisms that might facilitate opportunities for nations to learn from each other are few in number, fragmented, and often tend to duplicate efforts without seeking mutually helpful ways of co-operating. There is, therefore, a role for international agencies to provide leadership in this area by developing a suitable framework within which the best educational planners from many nations could share their knowledge and experience about planning the quality of education. In particular, there needs to be a great deal more sharing of information across nations concerning: the development of education information systems (especially the standardization of operational definitions for often-used indicators), the most efficient ways of deploying limited resources, and the most effective techniques for teacher pre-, in-, and on-service training.

Responding to the needs

Research

The first three needs described above (the need to reconceptualize what information is collected, the need to address major gaps in education information systems, and the need to establish appropriate information aggregation, scaling, and coverage levels) could all be addressed as part of a single co-ordinated research and development project. The project could be conducted in several countries and would be concerned with developing, trial-testing, and documenting procedures for the setting up of educational information systems that could be used to guide decisions aimed at improving the quality of education.

The research project could be developed in two stages. The first stage would consist of a detailed articulation of the essential steps that need to be taken, with each step being linked to a practical description of how an educational planner would undertake the work required. The second stage would demonstrate all of the steps covered in the first stage by applying them to case studies conducted in at least one developed and at least one developing country.

In summary, there would be eight main areas that would be addressed by this research project.

1. The identification of policy-related questions that are faced by decision makers (operating at different levels of an education system) when they are aiming to improve the quality of education.

2. The prioritization of these questions and precise linkage of them to potential future policy decisions at the appropriate decision-making level.

3. The use of these questions in order to: (i) identify what relevant information is available in existing data collections, (ii) indicate what new data need to be collected, (iii) eliminate redundancies due to overlaps in existing data collections, and (iv) terminate "traditional", but rarely-used data collections.

4. The review of the appropriate coverage level of the data collection (census or survey), the timeliness of the data collection (yearly or less frequently), and major gaps that are common in most data collections (especially information describing student educational achievement, student time spend on various curriculum offerings, student "tracking" patterns, teacher knowledge of subject matter, and unit cost measures).

5. The detailed specification of the indicators of the quality of education that will be assessed (including the provision and justification of construct names, operational definitions, computer-based coding systems, techniques and materials to be used to collect data, and detailed test blueprints in association with reliability and validity information).

6. The collection, analysis, and preparation of appropriate data according to acceptable scientific standards and the creation of appropriate data archives that will be readily accessible for later secondary analyses.

7. The analysis of the data using approaches that are appropriate for the questions posed and the backgrounds of the audiences who will receive the research reports (including the presentation of appropriate measures of sampling and measurement errors).

8. The linkage of suitable information dissemination procedures with both the policy questions posed initially and the decision-making levels at which the policy decisions will be taken (including the formulation and testing of new policy questions that emerge during the conduct of the data analyses).

Training

The fourth and fifth needs described above (the need for improved communication between educational planners and decision makers, and the need to ensure high technical standards for the collection, preparation, and analysis of data) could be addressed by setting up several training programs that will concentrate on "The Educational Planner as an Information Broker" and "The Educational Planner as a Technically Skilled Research Manager".

(a) The educational planner as an information broker

In order to develop a meaningful dialogue between educational planners and decision-makers there is a need for educational planners to undertake training in areas that have, until now, been considered to be "outside" the world of educational planning. At the centre of this kind of training programme would be an emphasis on communication skills that will facilitate responses to a variety of information needs and information formats. In essence, this training should enable the educational planner to become a broker between the decision-makers who require information in order to make informed policy decisions and the available information resources.

The notion of the "broker" is important here because it is expected that, in order to contribute towards improvements in the quality of education in the 1990s, the educational planner will extend his/her role beyond the matching of information requests with information, to a new era of pro-actively anticipating needs and opportunities, identifying and providing interpretations of technical trends, synthesizing themes and issues from large bodies of research evidence in a manner that can be acted upon, and exploring innovative ways of revealing and disseminating "the meaning behind the data". The content of a training program that will cover these areas will require courses to be prepared in two main areas.

(i) Applied policy development and analysis

In order for the educational planner to obtain some understanding of the decision-maker's world and thereby assist with the preparation and answering of important questions, training in policy development and analysis would be essential. This training should be carried out through a number of real-life examples of policy development and/or policy change at several decision-making levels within an education system. The teaching materials would need to centre upon the issues, pressures, constraints, and evidence taken into consideration by a key decision-maker leading up to, during, and after making an important decision aimed at improving the quality of education. These materials could include a range of items that played an influential role in these processes. For example, newspaper, television and/or radio coverage, government legislation, correspondence (especially from powerful individuals and lobby groups), informed commentaries, relevant research evidence, reactions by experts, postmortem investigations, and follow-up evaluations.

(ii) Information syntheses for policy-related decisions

The second important area of this training program would be in the preparation of systematic information syntheses that reach conclusions in terms that are accessible to decision-makers. The vital element here would be to move educational planners away from developing descriptive non-analytical information summaries and abstracts (whether they be in the form of tables of figures or summarized conclusions of research studies). Techniques such as "real" research review (that is, research synthesis and not research summarization), secondary analysis of important and relevant data sets, and meta-analysis, should form the main areas of study. These research reviews would be directed towards particular policy areas

167

and would need to conclude with clear-cut recommendations for action written in language that was accessible to decision-makers.

(b) The educational planner as a technically skilled research manager

The best-designed information systems in the world are worthless unless the data upon which they are based are collected, prepared, and analysed in a technically sound manner. The kinds of expertise required to ensure success in these areas are essentially the skills needed to conduct and manage high quality educational research. In an earlier chapter it was indicated that the content of an appropriate training program in this area had to be considered carefully in association with the way in which the training was delivered.

Training in this area should be centred around a set of "stand-alone" modules focussed on "basic research skills" (that should, at least, cover the areas of sample design, indicator specification, test and scale construction, data preparation, data analysis, and reporting) and "research management" (that should, at least, cover the areas of research design, the management of field work, the management of data coding and data entry teams, the development of data archives, and the selection and management of computer hardware and software).

The format of the training program would be based on a "hands on" teaching approach in which the theoretical aspects in the modules described above would be integrated with the conduct of a project nominated as a high priority project by the trainees' own countries. All of the training would simulate the experience of conducting a "real" moderately sized project - with the trainees (i) working as small teams, (ii) using state of the art technologies, and (iii) moving step-by-step through all project phases from the initial problem specification to the production of a final report that was of publishable standard. The depth and scope of this kind of training could not be covered in a short course of, say two to four weeks. The length of the course would be more in line with the time required to complete a reasonably substantial piece of educational research, say around one to one and a half years.

International co-operation

International agencies and institutions have a special role to play in responding to the need for more productive sharing of knowledge and experience concerning the best approaches to planning the quality of education. Several examples of how this might occur have been listed below.

(a) Co-ordination and/or initiation of research

International agencies could bring together various fragmented research activities in the international arena with a view to (i) documenting exactly what research is being undertaken, (ii) identifying the most valuable components of this work, and (iii) strengthening the resource-base of the high quality work that is being conducted so that *all* countries can share in the policy-related aspects of the research findings. These activities might be limited to the co-ordination of the research work that is already being undertaken, or they could extend to suggesting a research agenda for international bodies already working in the field, or they could include more direct intervention by commissioning and/or conducting appropriate research in this area.

(b) Improving the standards of regularly-collected information about the quality of education

International agencies such as the United Nations, the World Bank and the Asian Development Bank regularly make major policy decisions on the basis of indicators that purport to provide useful indicators of the quality of education. Many of these indicators are meaningless when used in a comparative sense because they are left to country-specific definitions that have little or no real validity. One important example of this is the definition of "literacy". In some countries a "literate person" is defined as a person who has completed four years of elementary schooling, whereas in other countries it is defined in terms of the opinion of the head of household during the collection of national census data. Both of these definitions have limited value because neither provides any "benchmark" information about the knowledge and skills that are required in order to be considered literate.

There are many other examples of often-used but poorly measured constructs in publications issued by International agencies. These all need to be reviewed and aligned with meaningful and valid operational definitions that can be applied in a range of political and cultural contexts. Naturally, this review should subject all data collections associated with this area to questions such as: Are these data worth collecting? Who is actually using them? For what purposes are they used?

Concluding comments

In most countries of the world there is a great deal of interest in planning the quality of education through informed decision-making. This book has sought to explore a range of key issues and challenges in this area, and also to bring forward a distillation of "fundamental needs" and some suggestions for courses of action through which these needs might be addressed.

Each of the courses of action that were described carry some merit in their own right. However, in order for sustained gains to be made in many countries, these approaches will need to be located within a co-ordinated program that is managed skilfully and funded at appropriate levels. It is quite unlikely that any single country or single aid agency would have either the resources or the cross-cultural perspectives required to support successful training, research, and international co-operation initiatives on the scale suggested here. What is required is a truly international effort with widespread participation by developed and developing countries, international organizations such as the United Nations, international development banks, and international and national development agencies.

All of the participants in the workshop at which this book was prepared believed that 1990, being both *International Literacy Year* and the year in which the world-wide conference on *Education for All* is to be held, represented a most propitious date to commence major international co-operation in this area. Hopefully, their optimism, taken in combination with their scholarly contributions to this book, will provide sufficient impetus to open a wider debate on the worth of embarking on such an undertaking.

References

Adams, R. S. (Ed.) (1978). *Educational planning: Towards a qualitative perspective,* Paris: International Institute for Educational Planning.

Al-Nouri, A.G. (November, 1989). *Issues and practices in planning the quality of education in Bahrain, Egypt and Qatar.* Area study presented at the IIEP International Workshop on Issues and Practices in Planning the Quality of Education, Paris.

Anderson, L., Ryan D. and Shapiro, B. (1989). *The IEA classroom environment study,* Oxford: Pergamon.

Aziz, A. (November, 1989). *Issues and practices in planning the quality of education in Malaysia and the Philippines.* Area study presented at the IIEP International Workshop on Issues and Practices in Planning the Quality of Education, Paris.

Bathory, Z. (November, 1989). *Issues and practices in planning the quality of education in Hungary.* Case study presented at the IIEP International Workshop on Issues and Practices in Planning the Quality of Education, Paris.

Beeby, C. E. (1969). Educational quality in practice. In C. E. Beeby (Ed.), *Qualitative aspects of educational planning,* (pp. 39-68). Paris: International Institute for Educational Planning, Unesco.

Beeby, C. E. (1979). *Assessment of Indonesian education: A Guide in Planning.* Wellington: New Zealand, Council for Educational Research in Association with Oxford University Press.

Boediono, (November, 1989). *Educational management information systems in practice - the Case of Indonesia.* Case study presented at the IIEP International Workshop on Issues and Practices in Planning the Quality of Education, Paris.

Boisivon, J.P. (November, 1989). *Issues and practices in planning the quality of education in France.* Case study presented at the IIEP International Workshop on Issues and Practices in Planning the Quality of Education, Paris.

Bourke, S.F., Mills, J.M., Stanyon, J., and Holzer, F. (1981). *Performance in literacy and numeracy: 1980.* Canberra: Australian Government Publishing Service.

Bower, T.G.R. (1977). *Pathways in development.* Paris: Organisation for Economic Co-operation and Development. Centre for Educational Research and Innovation.

Brickell, J. L. (1974). Nominated samples from public schools and statistical bias. *American Educational Research Journal, 11*(4), 333-341.

Casley, D.J. and Lury, D. A. (1981). *Data collection in developing countries.* Oxford: Clarendon Press.

Chapman, D.W., and Windham D.M. (1986). *The evaluation of efficiency in educational development activities.* Tallahassee, Florida: Improving the Efficiency of Educational Systems Project.

Cohen, D.M., March, J.G., and Olsen, J.P. (1972). A Garbage can model of organizational choice. *Administrative Science Quaterly. 17* (1).

Coleman, J.S., Campbell, E.Q., Hobson, C.J., McPartland, J., Mood, A.M., Weinfeld, F.D., and York, R.L. (1966). *Equality of educational opportunity.* Washington, DC: Department of Health, Education, and Welfare.

Coombs, P. H. (1975). A global university enterprise. In: Ontario Institute for Studies in Education (Eds.), *Education on the move.* Paris: The Unesco Press.

Cronbach, L., and Gleser G.C. (1965). *Psychological tests and personnel decisions.* (2nd ed.). Urbana: University of Illinois Press.

Dhingra, K. (November, 1989). *Issue and practices in planning the quality of education in India.* Case study presented at the IIEP International Workshop on Issues and Practices in Planning the Quality of Education, Paris.

Ekholm, M. (November, 1989). *Issues and practices in planning the quality of education in Sweden.* Case study presented at the IIEP International Workshop on Issues and Practices in Planning the Quality of Education, Paris.

Espinola, V. (November, 1989). *Issues and practices in planning the quality of education in Argentina, Chile and Colombia.* Area study presented at the IIEP International Workshop on Issues and Practices in Planning the Quality of Education, Paris.

Fuller, B. (November, 1989). *Speaking evidence and answers: But are governments and educators asking questions?.* Theme paper presented at the IIEP International Workshop on Issues and Practices in Planning the Quality of Education, Paris.

Fuller, B. (1990). *Growing-up modern: The western state builds third world schools.* New York: Routledge.

Gipps, C., and Goldstein, H. (1983). *Monitoring children: An evaluation of the assessment of performance unit,* London: Heinemann.

Grisay A., and Mählck, L. (November, 1989). *A review of some research studies and policy documents concerned with the quality of education.* Theme paper presented at the IIEP International Workshop on Issues and Practices in Planning the Quality of Education, Paris.

Hallak, J. (1989). The future of educational planning. *Prospects.* XIX(2), 165-167.

Hanushek, E.A. (1986). The economics of schooling: Production and efficiency in public school. *Journal of Economic Literature.* 24, 1141-1177.

Hartwell, Ash (1989). *The Information System for Basic Education - The Case of Bostwana.* Case study presented at the IIEP International Workshop on Issues and Practices in Planning the Quality of Education, Paris.

Heyneman, S.P., and Loxley, W.A. (1983). The effect of primary school quality on academic achievement across twenty-nine high- and low-income countries. *American Journal of Sociology.* 88 (6), 1162-1194.

Husen, T. (Ed.) (1967). *International study of achievement in mathematics. A comparison of twelve countries. Vols. I & II.* New York: John Wiley.

Jiyono, and Suryadi, A. (1982). The planning, sampling, and some preliminary results of the Indonesian 9th grade survey. *Evaluation in Education, 6* (1), 5-30.

Keeves, J.P., and Sellin, N. (1988). Multilevel analysis. In J.P. Keeves (Ed.), *Educational research: Methodology and measurement. An international handbook.* New York: Pergamon Press.

Kennedy, M. (1984).   How evidence alters understanding and decisions. *Educational Evaluation and Policy Analysis, 6* (3), 207-226.

Kish, L. (1965). *Survey sampling.* New York: Wiley.

Klees, S.J. (1986). Planning and policy analysis in education: What can economics tell us? *Comparative Education Review, 30* (4), 547-607.

Levin, H. M. (November, 1989). *Major issues in the planning and coordination of data collection for improving school quality.* Theme paper presented at the IIEP International Workshop on Issues and Practices in Planning the Quality of Education, Paris.

Levin, H.M. (1983). *Cost-effectiveness: A primer.* Beverly Hills, California: Sage Publications.

Lewin, K. (1988).   Planning for scientific and technological development. In: T. Husén and T.N. Postlethwaite (Eds.), *International Encyclopedia of Education, Supplementary Volume One.* Oxford: Pergamon Press.

Lockheed, M.E., and Verspoor, A. (1989). *Improving primary education in developing countries: A review of policy options.* Washington: The World Bank.

McGaw, B., Long, M.G., Morgan, G., and Rosier, M. *Literacy and numeracy in Victorian schools: 1988.*   Hawthorn, Victoria: Australian Council for Educational Research.

March J.G., and Simon, H.A. (1958). *Organizations.* New York: John Wiley and Sons.

Meyer, J., and Rowan, B. (1977).   Institutionalized organizations: Formal structure as myth and ceremony. *American Journal of Sociology,* 83, 340-363.

Morgan, G. (1979). *A criterion-referenced measurement model with corrections for guessing and carelessness.* Melbourne: Australian Council for Educational Research. (Occasional Paper, No. 13.).

Murname, R.J. (1987). Improving education indicators and economic indicators: The same problems? *Educational Evaluation and Policy Analysis. 9* (2), 101-116.

Mwiria, K., and Komba, D. (November, 1989). *Issues and practices in planning the quality of education in Kenya and Tanzania.* Area study presented at the IIEP International Workshop on Issues and Practices in Planning the Quality of Education, Paris.

National Assessment of Educational Progress (NAEP). (1986). *The reading report card: Progress toward excellence in our schools.* Princeton, N.J. : NAEP.

Organization for Economic Co-operation and Development (OECD). (1989). *Schools and quality.* Paris: OECD.

Pelgrum, H., and Warries, E. (1986). *IEA 1986: Activities, institutions, and people.* Enschede (Netherlands): International Association for the Evaluation of Educational Achievement.

Peters, R. S. (1969). Sociological comments on concepts of quality and quantity in education. In C. E. Beeby (Ed.) *Qualitative aspects of educational planning* (pp. 149-167). Paris: International Institute for Educational Planning, UNESCO.

Pfeffer, J., and Salancik, G. (1978). *The external control of organizations.* New York: Harper and Row.

Philp, H. The evaluation of quality in education. (1969). In C. E. Beeby (Ed.) *Qualitative aspects of educational planning* (pp. 280-291). Paris: International Institute for Educational Planning, Unesco.

Postlethwaite T. N., and Ross, K. N. (1987). *Indonesia: Quality and economics of education. Joint assignment report.* Jakarta: Ministry of Education and Culture.

Ross, K. N. (1985). Sampling errors. In T. Husen and T. N. Postlethwaite (Eds.), *The international encyclopedia of education* (pp. 4381-4385). New York: Pergamon.

Ross, K.N. (1986). *Sample design options for a multi-purpose survey of villages in Indonesia. Assignment report. August 1986.* Jakarta: Office of Educational and Cultural Research and Development, Ministry of Education and Culture.

Ross, K.N. (1987). Sample design. *International Journal of Educational Research, 11* (1), 57-75.

Ross, K.N., and Postlethwaite, T.N. (November, 1989). *Planning the quality of education: Some problems and issues associated with the sampling, collection, preparation, and analysis of data.* Theme paper presented at the IIEP International Workshop on Issues and Practices in Planning the Quality of Education, Paris.

Scott, W.R. (1981). *Organizations: rational, natural and open systems*. Englewood Cliffs, N.J. : Prentice-Hall.

Scriven, M. (1980). Self-referent research. *Educational Researcher. 9*, 7-11.

Scriven, M. (1983). Costs in evaluation: Concept and practice. In: M.C. Alkin and L.C. Solmon (Eds.) *The Costs of evaluation* (pp. 27-44). Beverly Hills: Sage Publications.

Sergiovanni, T.J., Burlingame, M., Coombs, F.S., and Thurston, P.W. (1987). *Educational governance and administration*. Englewood Cliffs, New Jersey: Prentice Hall.

Simon, H.A. (1945). *Administrative behavior.* New York: Macmillan.

Somerset, H.C.A. (1987). *Examination Reform in Kenya*, World Bank Discussion Paper, Education and Training Series, Report No. EDTG4. Washington: World Bank.

Somerset, H.C.A. (November, 1989). *The use of examination data for planning quality improvement.* Theme paper presented at the IIEP International Workshop on Issues and Practices in Planning the Quality of Education, Paris.

Staff, (1987). Los Angeles school achievement test scores. *Los Angeles Times* (Metro Supplement), 8 November, pp. 1-2.

Taylor, F.W. (1911). *Principles of scientific management.* New York: Harper and Brothers.

Tsang, M.C. (1988). *Cost analysis for educational policy-making: A review of cost studies in education in developing countries.* Cambridge, Mass.: Harvard Institute for International Development, Harvard University.

Tyler, R.W. (1986). Changing concepts of educational evaluation. *International Journal of Educational Research, 10* (1), 1-113.

Walker, D. (1976). *The IEA six subject study: An empirical study of education in twenty-one countries.* Stockholm: Almqvist and Wiksell/New York: Wiley.

Weber, M. (1945). Bureaucracy. In M. Weber, *Essays in sociology*, translated and edited by H.H. Gerth and C.W. Mills. London: Oxford University Press.

Weick, K. (1976). Educational organizations as loosely-coupled systems. *Administrative Science Quaterly*, 21, 1-19.

Weiss, C. (1980). *Social science research and decision-making.* New York: Columbia University Press.

Windham, D. (November, 1989). *EMIS development and planning the quality of education.* Theme paper presented at the IIEP International Workshop on Issues and Practices in Planning the Quality of Education, Paris.

Windham, D.M. (1988). Effectiveness indicators in the economic analysis of educational activities. *International Journal of Educational Research, 12* (6), 577-665.

Windham, D.M. (1990). The cost of effective schools. In P. Vedder (Ed.), *Fundamental Studies in Educational Research.* Amsterdam: Swets and Zeitlinger Publishers.

Appendix

Participants in the IIEP workshop on
Issues and practices in planning the quality of education,
Paris, 12-17 November 1989

Abdel Ghani AL-NOURI, Director of Planning, Ministry of Education, Doha, Qatar,

Arfah A. AZIZ, Director, Malaysian Language Institute, Kuala Lumpur, Malaysia

Zolthan BATHORY, Chief, Educational Evaluation Unit, National Institute of Education Budapest, Hungary

BOEDIONO, Head, Center for Informatics, Ministry of Education and Culture, Jakarta, Indonesia

Jean-Pierre BOISIVON, Director, Department of Evaluation and Future Oriented Studies, Ministry of National Education, Paris, France

Kiran DHINGRA, Deputy Secretary, School Division, Ministry of Human Resources Development, New Delhi, India

Mats EKHOLM, Director, National Training Programme of School Leaders, Linköping, Sweden

Viola ESPINOLA, Research Fellow, National Center for Educational Research and Documentation, Santiago, Chile

Bruce FULLER, Associate Professor of Education, Harvard University, Cambridge, Massachusett, USA

Dorothy M. GILFORD, Director, National Research Council, Washington, D.C., USA

Aletta GRISAY, Research Fellow, Department of Experimental Pedagogy, University of Liege, Sart Tilman, Belgium

Stephen P. HEYNEMAN, Chief, Human Resources Division, The World Bank, Washington, D.C., USA

Archie LAPOINTE, Executive Director, National Assessment of Educational Progress, Princeton, New Jersey, USA

Henry LEVIN, Director, Center for Educational Research, Stanford University, Stanford, California, USA

Marlaine LOCKHEED, Senior Education Sociologist, Education and Employment Division, The World Bank, Washington, D.C., USA

Kilemi MWIRIA, Research Fellow, Bureau of Educational Research, Kenyatta University, Nairobi, Kenya

T. Neville POSTLETHWAITE, Professor of Comparative Education, University of Hamburg, Hamburg, Federal Republic of Germany

Kenneth N. ROSS, Reader in Education, Deakin University, Geelong, Victoria, Australia

Anthony SOMERSET, Educational Research Consultant, University of Sussex, Falmer, Brighton, United Kingdom

Douglas M. WINDHAM, Professor of Educational Administration, State University of New York at Albany, Albany, New York, USA

Unesco Secretariat

Colin N. POWER, Assistant Director-General for Education

Gabriel CARCELES BREIS, Director, Office of Statistics

Etienne BRUNSWIC, Consultant

IIEP

Jacques HALLAK, Director

Lars MAHLCK, Programme Specialist

Achevé d'imprimer
sur les presses de l'imprimerie GAUTHIER-VILLARS
75018 PARIS